SCHOOLCRAFT COLLEGE LIBRARY

3 3013 00032 8769

WITH...

P9-AZU-583

Divorce and Remarriage

Religious and Psychological Perspectives

Edited by
William P. Roberts

Sheed & Ward

BV
838
.D58
1990

Copyright© 1990
William P. Roberts

All rights reserved. No part of this book may be reproduced or translated
in any form or by any means, electronic or mechanical, including photo-
copying, recording or by an information storage and retrieval system
without permission in writing from the Publisher.

Sheed & Ward™ is a service of National Catholic Reporter Publishing
Company, Inc.

Library of Congress Catalog Card Number: 89-63115

ISBN: 1-55612-231-4

Published by: Sheed & Ward
                115 E. Armour Blvd. P.O. Box 419492
                Kansas City, MO 64141-6492

To order, call: (800) 333-7373

Contents

Foreword v

1. Remarriage: Shaping the Pastoral Questions
   That Facilitate Life
   Paula Ripple 1

2. Eastern Orthodox Perspectives on Divorce and Remarriage
   John H. Erickson 15

3. The International Theological Commission and Indissolubility
   Theodore Mackin, S.J. 27

4. Sacramentality of Second Marriages
   Bernard Cooke 70

5. Remarriage and the Divorce Sayings Attributed to Jesus
   Mary Rose D'Angelo 78

6. Divorce and Remarriage: A Moral Perspective
   Margaret A. Farley, R.S.M. 107

7. The Consequences of Marital Breakdown
   Jack Dominian 128

8. Questions Concerning the Matrimonial Tribunals
   and the Annulment Process
   Ladislas Orsy, S.J. 138

About the Authors 156

Acknowledgments

First, I am very grateful to each of the speakers for participating in this three day symposium on divorce and remarriage, and for preparing the papers that appear in this book.

My special thanks go to the Marianists of the Cincinnati Province who provided the major grant that made the symposium possible. I thank also the following University of Dayton schools and offices that donated indispensable matching gifts: College of Arts and Sciences, Department of Religious Studies, Office of the Dean for Graduate Studies and Research, Office of the Provost, and the School of Education.

Finally, I express my sincere appreciation to my wife Challon for her help and support throughout the two years of preparation that went into the symposium, to my graduate assistants Mary Lynn Naughton and Joan McGuinness Wagner, and to Robert Heyer, editor at Sheed and Ward.

William P. Roberts

Foreword

A national symposium entitled "Divorce and Remarriage: Religious and Psychological Perspectives" was held in the Kennedy Union Ballroom on the campus of the University of Dayton, March 9-11, 1989. This symposium attracted 600 professional people from across the United States, and from Canada, England, and New Zealand. The participants, for the most part, consisted of canon lawyers, diocesan and parish level family life ministers, pastors, and religious educators. They came from diverse life styles: celibate, married, divorced, remarried. Present were leaders of the North American Conference of Separated and Divorced Catholics, the National Association of Catholic Diocesan Family Life Ministers, and the Marriage Research Committee of the Canon Law Society of America.

It may be no exaggeration to describe the atmosphere in that ballroom for those three days as "electrically charged" by a high level of interest, serious searching, and pastoral concern, as well as by a deep sense of pain and hurt experienced personally and/or vicariously by so many of the participants involved in ministry to the divorced and remarried. In a remarkably perceivable way the two worlds of academic scholarship and of pastoral reality were brought together into that room, and entered into profound dialogue with one another in a spirit of mutual respect, appreciation and shared passion. While there is no way to capture and translate into written word the dynamics of the interchange that took place, this book presents the papers that were prepared for the symposium by eight eminent scholars and professionals.

Theology is first and foremost a faith reflection on experience. In the first paper Paula Ripple, for two decades a leader in ministry to the divorced and remarried, reflects on the experience of divorced and remarried Catholics. Her paper also traces the history of this ministry as it is reflected through a change in the questions and a change in focus.

Sometimes we may forget that there is not one Catholic tradition in regard to divorce and remarriage, but two: the Eastern Orthodox as well as the Roman Catholic. Eastern Orthodox theologian John Erickson explores some of the historical circumstances in which Eastern law and practice regarding divorce and remarriage developed. His paper sheds light on the most characteristic elements of this tradition, and points to what he calls some of its "weaknesses and limitations."

Theodore Mackin, S.J., the nation's leading scholar on the Catholic theology of marriage, introduces his paper with a brief reflection on the Matthean version of Jesus' prohibition of divorce and a precis of Augustine's teaching on the indissolubility of marriage. The purpose of his essay is to examine the case made for indissolubility by the members of the Catholic Church's International Theological Commission in the late 1970's. Mackin presents a careful analysis of the propositions, commentaries, and working papers issued by the Commission on indissolubility. He concludes his essay with a series of critical reflections.

Noted theologian Bernard Cooke grapples with an issue that is quite related to the indissolubility question, namely, the sacramentality of marriage. What makes a marriage sacramental? Where does ecclesiastical legislation regarding the validity or invalidity of given marriages affect their sacramental effectiveness? Is it possible that a second marriage not approved by the church might be experienced as sacramental, while the first was not?

Mary Rose D'Angelo, a professor of New Testament Studies at Villanova University turns our attention to the divorce sayings attributed to Jesus. She reviews the sayings three times from different perspectives. First, she gives a brief description of the sayings and their relation to one another, stressing the variations among them. In her second review she raises the question of their origin. Her third review of the sayings examines their function in the context of the various works in which they appear. Here the author underlines the function of the sayings in early Christian asceticism.

In her paper, Margaret Farley, R.S.M., of Yale University Divinity School, reflects on divorce and remarriage from a moral perspective. She examines the meaning and purpose of commitment, and the criteria for continuing obligation or justified release from commitment. She then applies this thinking to the realities of marriage, divorce, and remarriage.

Much attention has been given over the last few decades to the reasons that justify divorce, and to the harmful effects of remaining trapped in a destructive marriage. This important focus, however, cannot be allowed to obscure the devastating and harmful effects that divorce has on both adults and children. Psychiatrist Jack Dominian describes these effects and cautions that we not look upon divorce as a panacea. Rather, we must recognize the high cost in human suffering of divorce, and make the prevention of marital breakdown one of the urgent priorities of Western society.

In the final paper noted canonist Ladislas Orsy, S.J., addresses questions regarding the matrimonial tribunals and the annulment process. He examines the objective values the tribunals are meant to serve, and the subjective dispositions in the judges which contribute to the genesis of judicial decisions. His paper then explores possible alternatives to the tribunals.

The Roman Catholic Church has served society well in its insistence on the value of the permanency of marriage. This is an ongoing mission incumbent on all of us. The question is whether, in our efforts to preserve the permanency of marriage, we have sometimes failed in our mandate to minister in a compassionate and healing way to those whose marriages are irretrievably lost. Can we discover a pastoral approach that better combines our commitment to marital fidelity with a more Christlike ministry to the divorced and remarried? To this end may the present volume make a small contribution!

William P. Roberts

1
Remarriage: Shaping the Pastoral Questions That Facilitate Life

Paula Ripple

My dwelling, like a shepherd's tent, is struck down and borne away from me. You have folded up my life, like a weaver who severs the last thread. Day and night you give me over to torment, I cry out until dawn . . . like a swallow I utter shrill cries; I moan like a dove. My eyes grow weak, gazing heavenward; O Lord, I am in sadness, be my strength. Isaiah 38:12-14.

"We live in one of the most marrying countries in the world." This is a statement that is often made about the United States (96% of women and 94% of men will marry during their lifetime). Despite the high divorce rates (45% for first marriages and 55% for second marriages), the vast majority of men and women continue to choose marriage as a way to live and to grow. Despite the high divorce rates, a recent poll of high school seniors reveals that most of them expect to marry and to stay married to one person for life. Despite the high divorce rates, God continues to call faithful people to the sharing of life in that community of life and love of which the Church speaks in Sections 47-52 in the Pastoral Constitution on the Church in the Modern World. And, perhaps most of all for those of us who are gathered here, despite the high divorce rates we are challenged to believe in and facilitate the fashioning of support systems for women and men who continue to embrace the ideal of permanence in a culture that offers disposability and replacement with such ease.

The rise in divorce rates which we have seen actually began not in the late 1960s but, rather, in the late 1860s—the period following the Civil War. This increase in the 1860s, as in the 1960s, was reflective of profound cultural, social and economic change. The increases which had been gradual skyrocketed in the late 1960s and early seventies and then plateaued. United States Census Bureau statistics tell us that the divorce rate dropped slightly in the mid '80s.

1

With the rapidity and persistence of changes which affect the American home and family, we must expect divorce rates to remain high. The fact that 67% of first marriages that end in divorce end within the first ten years is an ever-present challenge to us to continue to invest in both marriage preparation and marriage enrichment programs. Even more challenging to us and even more directly related to our subject matter here is the studied estimate that as many as 75% of divorcing Catholics either have or will remarry without annulments.

Can we allow ourselves to indulge the easy conclusion that these are persons for whom the Church is no longer important? Can we risk losing the gifts of these many men and women whose freedom to "belong" was lost first through the tragedy of divorce and subsequently through the often painful decision to remarry?

Setting the Context for Our Discussion Here

Water and oil are Christian symbols that become more sacred to baptized persons as they grow in the faith. Both are associated with baptism where we are cleansed with water and called to grow through our association with Jesus and then anointed with oil as an invitation to become a part of the Christian family. The importance of these symbols in terms of what they at once ask of us and offer to us is no less true for our divorced and remarried members.

In his Encyclical Familiaris Consortio (November 1981), Pope John Paul II offered the following reminder to the Christian community:

> . . . The Church, which was set up to lead to salvation all people and especially the baptized, cannot abandon to their own devices those who have been previously bound by sacramental marriage and who have attempted a second marriage. The Church will therefore make untiring efforts to put at their disposal her means of salvation.

> . . . I earnestly call upon pastors and the whole community of the faithful to help the divorced, and with solicitous care to make sure that they do not consider themselves as separated from the Church, for as baptized persons they can, and indeed must, share in her life . . . . Let the Church pray for them, encourage them and show herself a merciful mother, and thus sustain them in faith and hope. (Section 84)

In his striking portrayal of the responsibility of the Church to all who have been baptized into Christ and in his challenge to "make untiring efforts" to offer to them the "means of salvation," we are reminded that often the Church and its pastoral ministers feel caught in the tension that exists between seemingly irreconcilable ideals. In this context, the ideals of which we speak are those with which Jesus often wrestled, the ideals of permanence and compassion.

I believe that this discussion will be further enriched and expanded through the provision of some historical background with regard to the origins and development of divorce ministry.

The Divorcing Person in a Responding Church

My own roots in the journey with divorcing persons began back in 1972 when I met and listened to the story of a 23 year old man whose marriage had lasted only nine months. Since he was the first divorced person whose story I had ever heard, it was he who led me into an understanding of the divorce process, an understanding which will never be complete. His presence challenged every stereotype I had learned along the way; his story linked the divorce experience with the grieving process which I had come to understand through the works of Kubler Ross.

Two years later, in 1974, I met and began to work with Father Jim Young. I was present in Boston when the peer ministry network that has come to be known as the North American Conference of Separated and Divorced Catholics had its primitive beginnings. Structured on the same regional framework used by the National Council of Catholic Bishops, it was intended from the beginning that the system of support groups could function with and through already existing diocesan offices.

In those early years of struggle for finances and credibility for a ministry whose place in the Church was questioned, we could never have envisioned either the extent or the rapidity of the growth of this then fledgling grass roots movement.

In less than fifteen years, we have seen the number of diocesan offices grow from three in 1974 to nearly 75% of all dioceses at the present time. In less than fifteen years, the support group system has increased in strength, in numbers, and in the replacement of priests and sisters with divorced persons to staff diocesan offices of divorce ministry and, in some cases, to serve as advocates in Tribunal work.

My personal experience of this growth has been realized through a continuing education program for clergy of whose faculty I have been a part for twelve years. Father Jack Finnegan and I worked together in the early years. We would do back to back presentations, one on pastoral care for the separated and divorced and one on the canonical dimensions and the ministry of the Tribunal. In the early years, we were often questioned and it was sometimes with reluctance that our listeners accepted our information. Gradually, it was apparent that reluctance had given way to a need for developing an increased sensitivity to the pain and tragic circumstances of those seeking healing and help in the wake of a lost marriage. Last May, more than two thirds of the men in that program had worked with divorce groups and with retreat weekends as well as with seeking help through the tribunal system.

Truly, this was a ministry whose time had come. The changes are reflected not only through the different questions being asked by people in ministry. They are reflected also by a change in the inner attitudes out of which the pastoral questions are discussed. We seem much closer to the possibility of divorcing persons finding the home in the Church of which Robert Frost speaks in the Death of the Hired Man:

'Home is the place where, when you go there,
They have to take you in.'

'I should have called it
Something you somehow haven't to deserve.'

The History as it is Reflected Through a Change in the Questions

Whether or not all baptized persons can hope to experience the Church as a home is often reflected through the question out of which we approach a certain topic.

It is important to keep in mind that, all too often, we are dealing with the fact that answer-seeking is more paramount in people's minds than question-forming. Whether it is in search of sanctity or security, we are confronted with the truth that many good Christians want only a simple, direct and sure answer. It is a significant measure of growth in Christian maturity when any of us can let go of the instinctive desire each of us sometimes has for the answer, and then to move beyond that to scrutinize even the questions to be sure they are (1) our own and (2) actually related to what it is that we are wrestling with. Often, this means letting go of someone else's questions and allowing our own life-giving questions to form.

The questions we ask make a difference—sometimes, all the difference. Where we start does matter for it reveals a set of inner attitudes out of which the pastoral care we hope to offer will flow. The questions in the Church have changed since we began in 1972. They have changed for those in ministry, for all the members of the Christian community, and for divorcing persons themselves.

An important part of understanding the response of the Church to divorcing persons may lie in the realization that it was not just the Church that was asking the wrong questions. It was not just the Church that had not linked grieving to divorcing; not just the Church that did not have the keys to the long process of recovery that is the lot of every divorcing person.

It is only within the same last fifteen years that the secular counselling world has come to terms with the truth that divorce is not a lark experience, that divorce is devastating to the person and to the total network of relationships that are a part of the lives of both persons, their children and relatives.

The growth of divorce adjustment counselling in general has paralleled the growth of divorce ministry in the Catholic Church. Many believe that it is our ministry which has given leadership to this entire movement, in the Church and outside it.

Perhaps a part of the pain we experience when we remember the history of the Church in relationship to divorcing persons stems from our own idealism about the Church as our home and our expectation that it will have a heightened attentiveness to all forms of human suffering. We expect that it will set no one outside the family.

The questions that follow are, I believe, reflective of the changes in an approach to the devastating experience of divorce. The changes are reflected in both persons and in institutions.

1. The question is not: "What is wrong with all these careless divorcing people?" The question is: "How can we be present to and supportive of people who have experienced this human tragedy? How can we be faithful to our common baptismal commitment?"

2. The question is not: "Are we condoning divorce when we care about divorced persons?" The question is: "How do we respond to the tension that exists between two ideals presented to us so clearly by Jesus, the ideal of permanence in marriage and the ideal of compassion?"

3. The question is not: "Is divorce a sin and all divorcees sinners?" The question is: "How can we communicate the message of God's ever-present love to those who feel devastated and powerless in the wake of the loss of a marriage?"

4. The question is not: "If we allow men and women to come together in support groups, will they not meet, fall in love and want to marry? How can we prevent this?" The question is: "How can we offer a support system in which hurting people can heal, learn from the past and have the hope of one day forming life-nurturing relationships?"

5. The question is not: "How can we prevent people from remarrying?" The question is: "What can we do to call people to faithfulness to life so that, if and when they do remarry, they have the possibility of experiencing that community of life and love they either did not have before or had and lost?"

These questions are not reflective of all of the changes; they do provide some insight into where we have been and where we are now with regard to the history of divorce ministry. They also serve as a framework in leading us into some of the major concerns for the future of divorce ministry and pastoral care for those who have remarried or will do so in the future.

The History as It Is Reflected Through a Change in Focus

Just as the questions have changed with the ongoing growth and maturing of ministry to the separated, divorced and remarried, so, too, have the areas of focus shifted. We have seen some change in the energy investment in some areas and greater emphasis in others.

The earliest goal of the North American Conference of Separated and Divorced Catholics (which has always included our remarried brothers and sisters in the Christian community) was the support and healing of divorcing persons. It was the necessary place to begin; it also seemed like the most logical place.

The description given in Isaiah 38:12-14 could have been written by a divorcing person: "My dwelling is struck down . . . You have folded up my life, like a weaver who severs the last thread . . . O Lord, will you be my strength . . ."

It is only recently that the divorce experience has been articulated in any way that gives some insight into the terror and the intensity of the journey. Hurting persons are often unable to tell us that they hurt; they may lack clarity in sorting out the various elements of that pain as well as any knowledge of what to do.

One thing has grown clear to me since 1972. There is no human suffering equal to that of the loss of a relationship that has been central to one's life.

A comparison that I like to use is the following. A relationship is not like a coat we wear, something external to us and something, which if lost, leaves us as we were before purchasing it. If it were like a coat, then the divorce process would end in the divorce court, which it clearly does not. Divorce would be like an event: buying a coat, losing it; choosing a relationship, letting go of it.

I believe that a chosen and important relationship is rather like a tapestry that two people choose to weave together. This tapestry is not woven out of materials external to ourselves. Rather, it is woven out of the inner threads of each person. Who we are is invested in important relationships. And, as the story of the relationship is woven into that inner tapestry, it eventually becomes unclear which threads belong to each person. (This may be why one of the important agendas for a divorcing person is to rediscover a sense of who they are now that they are no longer a part of that other person. Reestablishing personal identity is not a simple process for the reasons we have just mentioned.)

As we began with listening to the painful journey sketched by divorcing persons, one of our first tasks was to use those stories in the articulation of some of the common elements of the journey through divorce.

This history of divorce ministry is reflected in and through the major areas of focus through the early beginnings, into the later years and, now, as we face the challenges of the present and those of the future.

Where the Energy Was Invested at the Beginning

1. The major focus was the personal recovery of the divorcing person. This included all aspects of education.

2. The fashioning of a support system through a network of self-help groups where divorcing persons ministered to one another, largely by sharing their stories and reaching out to one another.

3. General education was necessary in order to remove the rampant misinformation that had so plagued former generations of divorcing persons.

4. Seeking a place for divorcing persons in the Church which had been their home was our goal. Moving towards communicating a sense of belonging was not an easy challenge when the stereotypic statement, "Good Catholics don't get divorced" had been so well internalized by most of us.

Realizing that we were but touching the tip of the iceberg, the early efforts required sensitivity to the Christian community which had grown up with little or no understanding of the pain involved in the ending of a marriage.

Further Direction in a Rapidly Growing Ministry

With each succeeding year, the scope of the ministry widened. One of the challenges was the fact that, while new areas of need were continually emerging, there was no part of the ministry that could be considered completed. One of the gifts was that, as some divorcing people who had needed the ministry completed their homework, they stayed on to carry responsibility for others who were just beginning.

Some of the areas receiving additional attention were added. These included:

1. Increased emphasis on the children of divorce with special ministries beginning to encompass their hurts and needs. Few people realize, even today, that children speak of their parents' divorce as their own. They often say, "When I got divorced . . ."

2. Continuation of a working relationship with Tribunal personnel in order that divorcing people have a better understanding of the annulment process and a decreased fear of the many distorted ideas they have heard

somewhere. One example of this relationship between the North American Conference of Separated and Divorced Catholics and the Tribunals was a Seminar held in Washington, D.C. in 1981 which brought together canon lawyers and persons involved in divorce ministry in order to better support and understand our respective roles.

It deserves special emphasis here to underscore the fact that, from the very beginning, some of the most sensitive and energetic proponents of divorce ministry were many canon lawyers from all parts of the country. After all, it was often they who had been the first to listen to the stories of divorcing persons.

3. Gradual involvement increased in working with family life offices and diocesan offices responsible for marriage preparation and marriage enrichment programs. As with the canon lawyers, we found substantial support from many family life directors who made our ministry a special wing of their work long before it was common for a separate office of divorce ministry to be established by a bishop.

4. Weekend retreats such as the Beginning Experience began to flourish as retreat houses became involved in opening their facilities to these hurting members of the Christian community.

5. Every facet of writing needed to be done. When my own book, *The Pain And The Possibility,* was published in 1978, it was often the only book on resource tables for divorced Catholics. The production of tapes and videotapes was important to fill the seemingly insatiable desire of divorcing persons for self-help materials.

6. Families of divorcing persons began asking for help. Days for parents, grandparents, brothers and sisters were being requested.

7. Removal of the law of automatic excommunication for Catholics who remarry without an annulment took place in 1978. This removal represented the fruit of much hard labor and good leadership, and it brought in its wake a kind of softening of some of the difficult issues which faced us then and which continue to be a part of our concern.

Once again, as additional needs surfaced, we had an ever-increasing number of healed and healthy divorce recoverees who could take more responsibility for a burgeoning ministry.

Once again, we were aware that there was nothing we could leave behind. There will always be a need for support groups that cover what we call the "early recovery" stages even as others are ready to move on to a more advanced stage of putting the experience behind them and growing on to some new place that will allow them to reenter the mainstream of life in the Christian community.

It needs to be said that, with all this emphasis on support groups and special ministry, it is not and never was our intention to make "professional divorced Catholics" of those led to this ministry by human tragedy. The total energies of those who have fought for their right to remain Catholic can well serve the total Christian community.

Major Issues as We Move into the Future

It deserves to be mentioned again that none of us who were early pioneers in shaping and giving direction to this ministry could ever have envisioned that we could have moved so far so well in such a short time.

It has often been said that the changes in the emphasis on the outsides of marriage gave way to a new understanding of marriage as the emphasis shifted to the insides of marriage. It seems to me that this is true of what lies ahead for us as we look at some of the yet unattended areas or at areas that require greater focus from us.

With many adequate support systems well in place, we recognize that it is the inner geography of the divorcing person that invites us to rethink some old positions and to grow to some new ones.

Thousands of faithful people who have been a part of the widespread support system have done and are doing their homework. Many have invested heroic energy in their own process of healing and growth. They have grown as persons and many have also grown up in their faith. Many say that the Church became important to them at the time of their separation or divorce in a way they had not recognized at the time of their marriage. The home many experienced in their Church at the time of the most painful chapter in their lives is one from which they would never wish to be cut off. Thoughts of remarriage raise new questions and intensify the longing they have for the support and acceptance of that same home. It is precisely because the Church has responded so faithfully to the needs of divorcing persons that the honest and challenging questions regarding remarriage can no longer be ignored.

We know that there are millions of divorced/remarried Catholics living in faithful marriages, marriages which give credibility to the Church's teaching that marriage is a community of life and love. Conversations with them reveal tragic stories of families torn apart, brothers and sisters fearing to attend weddings, and sadness that is described as a "kind of pall that has plagued us through all these years."

Some of these remarriages took place before the grounds for an annulment were changed. Some of them took place outside the Church simply because of lack of information. Some are the result of attitudes that once prevailed, "You can't be divorced and Catholic."

Providing information about the nature of divorce has been and remains important. Continuing to sensitize the Christian community so that the sense of belonging for divorcing persons can grow even stronger is far from finished. Generations of children of divorce have a multitude of needs, some of them yet untouched. And the list grows longer.

We began at the beginning in the most logical place—with the divorcing person. The most difficult pastoral questions that lie ahead are in another place for they touch on structures, laws, discipline and taking seriously our own words about theresponsibilities we have to every baptized person—to every person who has shared the symbols of water and of oil.

Issues That Presently Claim Our Attention

This history we have sketched of divorce ministry is one of which we can well be proud. It has been our gift to be in a position of leadership for other churches and for the professional counselling community. The unattended issues, those that face us as we look at the present and the future are not necessarily new. They do give indications of the course that lies ahead for us if we are to respond to the lives of faithful persons who understand well the costly demands of Christ's call to permanence as well as the challenges of belonging to a Church that values community.

1. As was mentioned above, the provision of a home for those already remarried remains with us. Many of them would return to a Church they no longer recognize. Yet they, like ourselves, have been baptized into Christ.

2. There are large numbers of persons who have sought annulments who have discovered, for a variety of reasons, that this form of ministry does not fit their particular situation. (A 90 year old man who wished to remarry could not even remember where he was married, had no family,

no available witnesses.) Yet they, like ourselves, seek a way of life that offers the possibility of happiness in their chosen state.

3. My own experience and that of friends who work in Tribunals reveals increasing numbers of persons who say they would never seek an annulment. For some, this may represent a lack of information regarding that process. For some, it is a conviction that their first marriage was sacramental. But, for others, this refusal to seek an annulment is born after a full exploration of the meaning and the possibility of that process. Yet they, like ourselves, want to know that no doors to new life have been automatically closed to them.

4. From the beginning, I have heard canon lawyers, in speaking of the annulment process, say that it answers one set of questions while raising others. During the past few years the questions being raised are changing. Significant numbers of people face painful family situations when adult children, having had the process carefully explained to them, are thrust into great turmoil when the marriage of their parents is annulled. These parents are filled with sadness that the possibility of happiness in a new marriage cannot be fully celebrated. They, like ourselves, want to share that happiness with family members who are closest to them.

5. Many divorcing people go back to the time of the marriage as the beginning of the divorce process. For them, the question of sacramentality is often easily dealt with. But large numbers of people say they had a good marriage, as good as anyone's, and that something else happened. The reality of failed friendship, of loss of relationship for all kinds of personal reasons and cultural factors, is at the heart of the divorce experience for them. They, like ourselves, often ask, "Why is divorce the unforgivable sin? Why must I be punished for a loss that has been so painful?" And they, like ourselves, simply want to be believed, to be looked upon as persons of sincerity and of faith.

To quote again the words of the Holy Father, "The Church cannot abandon to their own devices those who have been previously bound by sacramental marriage . . ."

Conclusion

For there is hope for a tree,
if it be cut down, that it will sprout again
and that its roots will not cease.

> Though its roots grow old in the ground,
> yet at the scent of water, it will bud,
> and put forth branches like a young plant. Job 14:7-9

When we began working with divorcing persons in 1972, the need was for external systems—self-help groups, pastoral people sensitized and educated regarding the divorce process, efficient tribunals seeking to fulfill their important role in facilitating life. Because of the response of the Church, there is now a need for what can only be called spiritual direction as people who are coming of age in their faith discern the truth of their lives as Christians cleansed in the healing waters of baptism and anointed with oil to the sharing of life. For some persons called to marriage in the first place, the ideals of a committed Christian life are not separable from their desire to marry again.

When the law of automatic excommunication for remarriage without an annulment was removed in 1978, a law that had come into existence following the Civil War, the statement was made: "This is an invitation to divorced remarried Catholics to come home. It is an invitation for them to seek caring pastoral help."

The law was removed at the request of the United States Bishops and its removal had an import unnoticed by many and not clearly measurable. It was clearly a "scent of living water" (Job 14) which held the promises of healing and hope.

It was painful then to ask the questions: "But, to what sort of home? To what level of participation? To what quality of love?"

The words of hope offered again in Familiaris Consortio hold that same "scent of water" to lives that have been "cut down" and yet long to "put forth branches like a young plant" (Job 14-7-9).

The words from the Holy Father's 1981 Encyclical quoted earlier are followed immediately with words that limit and caution:

> . . . They should be encouraged to listen to the word of God, to attend the Sacrifice of the Mass, to persevere in prayer, to contribute to works of charity and to community efforts in favor of justice, to bring up their children in the Christian faith, to cultivate the spirit and practice of penance, and thus implore, day by day, God's grace . . . However the Church reaffirms her practice, which is based on Sacred Scripture, of not admitting to the

Eucharistic Communion divorced persons who have remarried. (Section 84)

In a Church where so much of our current theological emphasis is Eucharist-centered, it becomes more and more difficult for divorcing persons who found in the Church a home for their healing and experienced the significance of being nourished by the Eucharist to hear such conditional love offered by that same Church when either the possibility or the reality of remarriage is raised.

How can we continue to call baptized persons to the ideal of unconditional love while, at the same time, setting such limits on the love offered them?

People whose marital home has been "struck down and borne away" (Ezekiel 38:13), the threads of whose tapestry of life has been "severed to the last thread" (Ezekiel 38:13) have trusted us with their lives and we were not found wanting in either compassion or reconciliation.

By reason of their baptism, they are linked with the cleansing and life-giving water. Bonds were formed then that needed no prior defense. Bonds strengthened through the tragedy of the loss of a marriage ought need no future defense.

Challenging as it may yet be for those of us gathered here and for all members baptized into Christ, we are called to be as water bearers, offering that "scent of water" that can hold out the hope of new life in an environment that heals and strengthens by the simple act of believing in the life stories of other believers as told to us by them.

2
Eastern Orthodox Perspectives on Divorce and Remarriage

John H. Erickson

The position of the Eastern Orthodox churches on divorce and remarriage is frequently referred to in Western discussions of the subject, but less often is it correctly understood. An older generation of Roman Catholic controversialists regarded the Orthodox as regrettably lax in matters of divorce. More recently those calling for changes in Catholic policies toward the divorced have appealed to the East's more "pastoral approach." Yet seldom have such discussions taken into consideration the very different historical circumstances in which Eastern law and practice developed. As a result, the deepest and most characteristic insights of the Eastern Orthodox have been inadequately explored, while at the same time weaknesses and limitations have been either ignored or misconstrued.

During the Middle Ages, in the course of its own historical development, the Latin Church slowly developed the notion that marriage is essentially a non-voidable contract which, if *ratum* and *consummatum*, persists until the death of one of the partners, remaining by definition indissoluble even if in fact the partners no longer show any signs of being husband and wife. In the words of the new Latin *Code of Canon Law*, "A ratified and consummated marriage cannot be dissolved by any human power or for any reason other than death" (canon 1141). Though even today in the West this understanding of marriage is widely regarded as axiomatic, unchanging and unchangeable, an Eastern Christian, at least in antiquity and in the earlier Middle Ages, would have had difficulty grasping it. For example, he would not have accorded to sexual relations—*a fortiori* to the first sexual act in marriage—a significant role in the formation of marriage. He also would have had difficulty conceiving of marriage as such as unconditionally indissoluble. At the same time, he might well have been shocked at the suggestion that Christian marriage is unconditionally dissolved by death, only "till death do us part." How is his apparently contradictory

15

reaction to be explained? A complete answer to this question would require careful examination of the development of marriage doctrine in the Christian East, and above all, the interraction of those components which entered into the development of marriage doctrine in both East and West: Roman law, and Christian tradition as expressed preeminently in Scripture and its interpretation.[1] For an appreciation of the distinctiveness of the Eastern approach, however, and of its possible significance for the issues of divorce and remarriage as they emerge in our own day, a thematic approach may prove more fruitful.

"From the Beginning . . ."

"Have you not read that he who made them from the beginning made them male and female . . .?" (Mt 19:4). This passage is perhaps the most frequently quoted in Eastern Christian discussions of marriage—quoted more frequently even than Eph 5:32, "This is a great mystery, and I take it to mean Christ and the church." The passage was used, first of all, to defend marriage, established "from the beginning," in paradise before the Fall, against any Marcionite or Encratite disparagement of the essential goodness of creation and sexuality. But, as patristic exegesis of the sequel to these words—"and the two shall become one flesh"—indicates, marriage is not simply divinely sanctioned animality. In the beginning God created them male and female—"co-being," to use the lapidary expression of Cyril of Alexandria—precisely so that they, in creaturely forms, might reflect and participate in the uncreated life of God the trinity, a life of perfect openness, of personal communion, of complete sharing, mutual interiority and mutual indwelling.

This is the vocation of marriage "from the beginning," and even after the Fall, something of paradise remains. "When husband and wife cleave to each other in love, there is a remnant of paradise," says Chrysostom (Hom. 20, on the writ of divorce, PG 51:221). Even after the fall, after man and woman exchange being for having, true personhood for self-absorbed and self-sufficient individualism, marriage remains their most immediate possibility for transcending autonomous natural necessity through self-giving love. Marriage therefore is not just a remedy against concupiscence, tolerated and legitimized in view of certain natural, utilitarian ends: procreation of children, maintenance of the family and other social institutions . . . It does not exist to serve the "common good" as distinct from the "particular." When Eastern writers like Chrysostom try to identify and order the aims of marriage, they begin with the "subjective," the nuptial community itself, rather than with the "objective," procreation:

> There are two reasons why marriage was instituted: to make us chaste and to give us children. Of these two reasons, the first takes precedence . . . especially now that the human race has filled the entire earth. At first the procreation of children was desirable, so that each might leave a memorial of his own life. There was not yet any hope of resurrection, but rather death held sway, and those who died thought that they would perish utterly after this life. Therefore God gave them the comfort of children . . . . . But now that the resurrection is at hand, and we do not speak of death but rather advance toward another life better than the present one, the desire for posterity is superfluous (Hom. 19, on marriage, PG 51:213)

To be sure, having children does provide obvious opportunities for liberating self-sacrifice, as the Fathers noted in their commentaries on I Tim 2:15—"woman will be saved through bearing children." But here too marriage is seen ultimately as a summons to true personal freedom, not just a divinely sanctioned way for perpetuating the species. Like consecrated virginity, to which it is so often compared, marriage "from the beginning" points to the Kingdom, where biological bonds and natural affinity are transcended by the immediacy of loving personal relationship.[2]

Interpreted in this eschatological light, Mt 19:4 not only situates the institution and meaning of marriage within the order of creation. It also affirms that perfect and *perpetual* monogamy is the norm of marriage, that for those who believe in the resurrection married love transcends even the necessity of death itself. The second-century apologist Athenagoras sums up what was to remain the widespread feeling of the Christian East: "He who rids himself of his first wife, even if she be dead, is an adulterer in disguise because he transgresses the hand of God, for in the beginning God created but one man and one woman" (*Supplication* 33, PG 6:968). The Great Church was to distance itself from heretical groups which altogether prohibited remarriage even for widowed spouses. It did not forget that Paul had even encouraged young widows to remarry. At the same time, remarriage was not held in high esteem. It was a concession to human weakness or natural necessity, not marriage as it had been established "from the beginning," the earthly image of the perfect covenant relationship of God and His people, of Christ and the Church. "Second marriages are not to be condemned," says Epiphanius, "but held in less honor." More pointed is Gregory of Nazianzen: "A first marriage is in full conformity with the law; the second is tolerated by indulgence; the third is noxious. But he who exceeds this number is plainly a swine" (Or. 37.8, PG 36:292).

In the East, those entering into second or third marriages were subjected to penance—one or two years for bigamists, up to five years for trigamists according to Basil the Great, whose "canonical epistles" were incorporated into Eastern canon law collections from the sixth century onward (canon 4). But if, in Basil's words, even a third was not really marriage, but "polygamy, or rather restricted fornication," what of fourth marriage? The Eastern Church rejected fourth marriage completely, even though some Christians, like the unfortunate Emperor Leo VI at the beginning of the tenth century, might attempt it. Having lost three wives without issue, he married a fourth time in the hope of gaining a legitimate heir, thus touching off one of the most protracted and bitter disputes in Byzantine history and also the first major quarrel between East and West on marriage matters— for Rome by this point did not scruple successive marriages. The Tome of Union, which ended this "tetragamy affair" and remains even now the last word on the subject for the Eastern Orthodox, utterly prohibited fourth marriage henceforth and allowed third marriage only for those under age forty, with no children from their previous unions—and then with a heavy penance.

". . . except for unchastity"

If in the Eastern Christian tradition Mt 19:4 was the point of departure for reflection on marriage, this text was not considered apart from Mt 19:8-9: The law allowed divorce, "but from the beginning it was not so. And I say to you, whoever divorces his wife except for unchastity (*porneia*), and marries another, commits adultery." The problem of the significance of these words in their Matthean context cannot be examined here. Very possibly Matthew used the exceptive phrase here and in 5:32 having in mind Old Testamental texts like Jer 3:1 (LXX—"If a wife shall be with another man, she shall not return to her husband, but being polluted she remains polluted") and Prov 11:22 (LXX—"He who keeps an adulterous wife is foolish and impious"). In any case, Basil the Great in his "canonical epistles" links Mt 19:9 with these texts and concludes that a man not only may but *must* divorce a wife guilty of *porneia* (canon 9, cf. 21). The same attitude can be seen in canon 8 of the Council of Neocaesarea: a cleric whose wife has committed adultery "must put her away; but if he retain her he can have no part in the ministry committed to him." For the East generally, the Matthean exceptive phrase is understood not as a derogation from the prohibition to divorce but as its logical and necessary corollary. Adultery is the antithesis of marriage as it was established "from the beginning": the perpetual union in love of one man and one woman. In the words of the nineteenth-century Russian lay theologian Alexei Khomiakov, "The holy union instituted by the Creator cannot be dissolved without sin by the human will; but the sin of adultery dissolves it, because adultery is its direct negation. The man who has become just another man in the eyes of his wife, the woman who has become just another woman in the eyes of her husband, are no longer and can no longer be husband and wife in the eyes of the Church."[3] Given this understanding of Mt 19, one can easily understand why an Eastern Christian like Khomiakov would term the Roman concept of indissolubility a "civil servitude." "The idea of organic and mutual union, that is, the inner sanctity of the conjugal state has disappeared."[4]

From the foregoing it is evident that the Eastern Orthodox Church does not just "tolerate" divorce. In some cases it may even counsel it. John Chrysostom gives an obvious example: "Better to break a marriage for righteousness' sake" than be forced "into some immoral act on the grounds of marriage" (Hom. 19 on I Cor, PG 61:155). Yet as anyone who has experienced the phenomenon of "codependence" can testify, divorce can be as hard as continued "marriage," so strong are the bonds forged by fallen nature. Little wonder that the disciples remark, "If such be the case of a man with his wife, it is not expedient to marry" (19:10). We are at once reminded that "Not all can receive this saying" (19:11). Byzantine commentators read Mt 19:9 in the light of Mt 5:32, where the prohibition of divorce along with the exceptive clause is set in the course of the Sermon on the Mount. It was seen as an example of Christ's fulfillment of the Law (5:17), of the radical righteousness to which Christ's followers are summoned. It was an ethical demand, a challenge to constant personal struggle against sin, not just as a new and tougher legal prescription.

"... without a valid reason ..."

In the event that monogamous marriage was destroyed by the sin of adultery, divorce without remarriage was regarded as the norm for Christians. "Some have made themselves eunuchs for the sake of the Kingdom of heaven" (Mt 19:12). Yet this did not altogether exclude the possibility of remarriage—as though "divorce" here meant only separation from bed, board and dwelling but *manente vinculo*, as some Roman Catholic theologians have maintained. In the Byzantine East, heir to the ancient world's concepts and assumptions concerning marriage, the notion of separation as distinct from divorce, or that marriage is by definition indissoluble, remained quite alien for many centuries.

In classical Roman law, marriage was regarded as a factual situation, not as a legal abstraction. It came into existence and continued to exist by the will of partners having the legal capacity for marriage, the *ius connubii*. Withdrawal of the *affectio maritalis* by one or both brought about its dissolution as surely as death did. Divorce whether for serious cause or simply by mutual consent therefore was common in classical times, as was subsequent remarriage.

The early Church did not attempt to replace this civil legal institution with one of its own. "Each of us regards as his the woman whom he married according to your laws," says the apologist Athenagoras (*Supplication* 33, PG 6:968). To be sure, the Church did not lose sight of its own standards when dealing with Christians. Thus it apparently was able to see marriage as blessed by God "in the beginning" in the stable, monogamous unions even of those who lacked the *ius connubii* (e.g., slaves) and who therefore were incapable of legal marriage. So also it denounced most forms of divorce as "simply contrary to our laws, even if the Romans judge the matter otherwise" (Gregory of Nazianzen, Ep. 144, PG 37:248). Yet bishops and other churchmen did not question whether divorce and subsequent remarriage was possible by postulating the unconditional indissolubility of matrimony. Patristic and conciliar texts dealing with marriage show signs of hesitation and occasional disharmony, but there is ample evidence of Christians being permitted to remarry after divorce. It is enough to cite the very explicit testimony of Epiphanius:

> He who cannot keep continence after the death of his first wife or who has separated from his wife for a valid motive, such as fornication, adultery, or some other misdeed, if he takes another wife, or if the wife takes another husband, the divine word does not condemn or exclude him from the Church or Life, but rather tolerates this on account of his weakness. Not that this man can keep two wives in his home, the first one still hanging around him. But if he is actually separated from his first wife, he may

take another according to the law if this be his desire. (*Panarion*, heresy 59, PG 41:1025)

The general direction of the Eastern canonical tradition is clear. While remarriage after divorce is discouraged, just as any remarriage is, restoration to communion without separation from the second spouse is possible not only for the "innocent" party but even for the "guilty," as canon 87 of the Synod in Trullo (691) later provides, though in his or her case only after an appropriately severe penance.

While the establishment of Christianity did not result in a revolution in the Roman law of marriage, there were efforts to check its more objectionable aspects, chief among them being divorce simply by mutual consent. In part this was done by exhortation—as the letters and sermons of churchmen like Basil the Great, Gregory of Nazianzen and John Chrysostom show so clearly. In part it was done by insisting that divorce was unacceptable "without a valid reason" (Trullo canon 87, cf. Basil canons 7, 35, 77). In fits and starts the civil law also tried to limit divorce by tying it to certain specific causes. Justinian in particular was motivated by the idea that "divorce must be the exclusive result of reasonable causes, expressly stated in law,"[5]—an idea which was to become a basic principle in later Byzantine jurisprudence. Those divorcing without a valid cause were subject to heavy penalties, at first monetary fines, but under Justinian, compulsory entrance into monasticism. But divorce by mutual consent lingered for centuries, despite the efforts of Justinian and later legislators; and Justinian's attempt (Novella 134) not only to forbid and penalize divorce without valid cause but to decree it null and void was altogether unsuccessful.

The Byzantine "symphony"

The Roman law tradition never died in Byzantium. Indeed, it was self-consciously maintained. But it was slowly transmuted through contact with Christian principles. The Byzantine ideal of "symphony" between *imperium* and *sacerdotium* assumed the concordance of civil law and church law—hence the most characteristic expression of the Byzantine canonical tradition, the *nomocanon*, which conveniently arranged civil *nomoi* and ecclesiastical *kanones* by topic. But if the "conductor" of this Byzantine symphony was the emperor, the melody being played became more and more distinctly Christian. When contradictions between laws and canons were detected, the canons at least in theory took precedence; when the civil laws were revised, passages deemed incompatible with the views of the Church were omitted. In divorce matters the "valid reasons" enumerated by the civil law were reduced to two types: those which could be assimilated to death (disappearance with presumption of death, permanent insanity, monastic habit, episcopal consecration . . .) and those which could be assimilated to adultery, which thus could be interpreted in the light of the Matthean exceptive clause (endangering the life of the spouse, secret abortion, forcing the spouse to prostitution . . .), i.e., serious assaults on the moral and spiritual foundations of marriage. At the same time, canonists freely made use of concepts and terminology drawn from Roman law. The Roman jurist Modestinus' definition of marriage as "a union of a man and a woman, and a sharing of the whole of life (*consortium omnis vitae*), a participation in divine and human laws," is repeated again and again in Eastern manuals of theology and canon law down to our own century but developed in a thoroughly Christian direction. The same holds true of Ulpian's dictum that "it is consent and not sexual relations that makes marriage," the emphasis shifting from will to love.[6]

Particularly significant for the later history of marriage in the Christian East were developments touching on the formation of the marital bond. In general the early Church had been more concerned about the character of Christian marriage than about the wedding. In time, diverse non-Christian rituals like crowning were given a Christian interpretation, and wedding festivities were often graced with the presence of Christian priests. Yet this initially had nothing to do with legal requirements. Only in the eighth century is ecclesiastical blessing officially recognized as one of the legal ways for establishing a marriage—and then only as an alternative for the lower classes. But the custom of an ecclesiastical blessing took hold, and in the early tenth century Emperor Leo VI issued his Novella 89:

> . . .we order that marriage be confirmed by the evidence of a sacred blessing. Therefore, if those who want to get married do not comply with that procedure, from its inception this union shall not be considered as marriage, and such a cohabitation will not produce legal effects.[7]

On the one hand, this decree gave the Church a virtual monopoly in marriage matters. Invested with exclusive responsibility for giving legal status to marriages—and divorces—the Church was able to enforce its own standards much more vigorously than ever before—as Emperor Leo himself would soon find out during the tetragamy affair. At the same time, the distinction between marriages conforming to the Church's norm and those merely tolerated out of condescension to human frailty was blurred. The Church ended up blessing marriages which at least in principle entailed a period of excommunication—the second and third marriages of the widowed and divorced who previously would have had recourse to a civil ceremony. In principle, a distinction was maintained. For example, a separate and distinct Rite of Second Marriage, penitential in tone, was composed. Yet very quickly the rationale for much of the early Church's discipline in marriage matters was forgotten. For example, Neocaesarea canon 7 had forbidden a priest to be present for the wedding banquet of persons entering a second marriage—obviously because this would seem hypocritical in the case of a marriage that entailed excommunication and that could not receive an ecclesiastical blessing. By the twelfth century, however, the commentator Aristenus interprets the canon as meaning that the priest who blesses the marriage cannot attend the reception.[8]

Marriage and Divorce Today

If the surviving accounts of marriage cases are any indication, Byzantine marriage law—that symphony of Roman and Christian elements—functioned reasonably smoothly and effectively. A sign of its strength and resilience may be the fact that it continued to operate without serious problems through most of the Orthodox world after the fall of the Byzantine Empire. Only in our own century has the symphony ended. Intimate links between Church and State, Christianity and society can no longer be taken for granted. The Church is left with the difficult task both of addressing problems unanticipated in the old nomocanonic system and of modifying elements in it which have in fact become dysfunctional. Confronted with this new situation, the Church faces many temptations. Instead of communicating its own deepest insights about marriage to the world of today, it could end up woodenly maintaining all the external forms and requirements of a bygone age, whether civil or ecclesiastical, and in the very process capitulate to an understanding of marriage quite at odds with Christian teaching.

Part of the present difficulty can be traced to the Byzantine requirement that a marriage must receive a priestly blessing in order to be valid. As in the Latin Church after Trent, attention in matrimonial cases tended to shift from the content of Christian marriage to the required form, from the capacity and commitment of the couple themselves to external elements which can be more easily introduced as evidence in a court of law. Complicating the Eastern situation further was the influence of Western scholastic principles of sacramental theology from the thirteenth century onward. Marriage is fitted rather awkwardly into the system of seven sacraments, and its proper minister is identified: but as the priest, and not—as the Latins maintained—the couple themselves.

It is understandable why, in the unitary Byzantine and post-Byzantine world, avoidance of ecclesiastical blessing could be regarded as tantamount to rejection of Christian teaching on marriage. But in the pluralistic world of the twentieth century, can we seriously maintain that marriages blessed by an Orthodox priest in the Orthodox Church according to the Orthodox Rite of Matrimony necessarily "count," while those not so blessed do not? Yet this is what some of the Orthodox churches today attempt to do. Converts to Orthodoxy are encouraged—or even required—to be remarried in a church wedding. Men married, divorced and remarried anywhere "outside" the Orthodox church may become candidates for ordination because the impediment of sequential bigamy, which traditionally has been taken very seriously by the Orthodox, is not considered to be present in their case. The list of anomalies could go on and on. To be sure, other Orthodox churches—most notably the Russian—take quite a different approach. For example, they grant dispensations from form in certain cases, and they "count" marriages entered into "outside" the Church provided that the qualities which the Church requires of marriage are present. Such contradictory practices suggest how confused the Orthodox understanding of marriage has become since the end of the Byzantine symphony.

Many other contemporary problems could be enumerated. How, for example, are the marriages of persons who in fact are non-religious agnostics to be regarded, even though these may have been blessed by an Orthodox priest in the Orthodox church according to the Orthodox Rite of Matrimony? Or what consideration should be given to psychological factors which might adversely affect a couple's capacity to relate to each other as husband and wife? The nomocanonic system allowed divorce but virtually ignored the concept of nullity. In these and many other areas, deeper reflection is urgently needed.

In his massive study of *Divorce and Remarriage*, Theodore Mackin observes that a chief concern of the fathers of the early Church "was to get Christian spouses to see their marriages not as liaisons become marriages sanctioned by Roman law, but as relationships of respect and caring love designed by God."[9] In our post-Christian age we face much the same challenge, save that now our own ecclesiastical forms may be among the obstacles which hinder a deeper understanding of Christian marriage. Fortunately the Orthodox tradition does offer many resources for this task: a firm but sensitive understanding of penitential discipline, a history of liturgical creativity, a tradition of openness to culture and to the problems of society, an approach to the sacraments not entirely imprisoned in scholastic theories, a pastoral theology solidly grounded in dogmatic theology, stressing the ultimate significance of personhood . . . Our greatest challenge may simply be in allowing these resources to become more than reminders of a glorious past and applying them to the needs of our own time and place.

Notes

1. See N. van der Wal, "Secular Law and the Eastern Church's Concept of Marriage," *Concilium* 5.6 (London, May 1970) 76-82; O. Rousseau, "Divorce and Remarriage: East and West," *Concilium* 24 (New York, April 1967) 119-38; J. Dauvillier and C. de Clerq, *Le mariage en droit canonique oriental* (Paris 1936); and especially the very erudite recent studies of P. L'Huillier, "The Indissolubility of Marriage in Orthodox Law and Practice," St. *Vladimir's Theological Quarterly* 32 (1988) 199-221, "L'attitude de l'Eglise Orthodoxe vis-à-vis du remariage des divorces," *Revue de Droit Canonique* 29 (1979) 44-59, and "Novella 89 of Leo the Wise on Marriage: An Insight into its Theoretical and Practical Impact," *Greek Orthodox Theological Review* 32 (1987) 153-62.

2. Among modern recent Orthodox writers on these themes see especially P. Evdokimov, *The Sacrament of Love* (St. Vladimir's Seminary Press, Crestwood, NY 1985); C. Yannaras, *The Freedom of Morality* (St. Vladimir's Seminary Press, Crestwood, NY 1984) 157-72; and also the studies of J. Meyendorff, *Marriage: An Orthodox Perspective* (St. Vladimir's Seminary Press, Crestwood, NY 1975) and H. T. Stylianopoulos, "Toward a Theology of Marriage in the Orthodox Church," *Greek Orthodox Theological Review* 22 (1977) 249-83.

3. *L'Eglise Latine et le Protestantisme au point de vue de l'Eglise d'Orient* (Lausanne 1872) 154.

4. *Ibid.* Cf. the comments of Evdokimov, p. 188: "A person who betrays his love betrays himself. But this need to remain on the level of the spirit can never be formalized or decreed. Love, like martyrdom, cannot be imposed on someone. The promise of fidelity is borne on the deepest realities of human life and on transactional realities. It is not imposed from without but raised from within, from the heart's dimension, and is addressed to the freedom of the spirit like an invitation to a banquet and a call to suffering. The act of faith enters into it, and one's fidelity comes alive in accordance with the integrity of one's faith. Within this mystery no one is judge except God, to whom the promise is made, and the conscience of the one who made the promise. If faith changes, fidelity also changes; it ceases to be a grace and it becomes a constraint." Evdokimov sums up the Orthodox position in this way (p. 189): "In permitting divorce, the Orthodox Church shows its infinite respect for the person and for the sacrament of charismatic love."

5. L'Huillier, "Indissolubility," 209.

6. Cf. the understanding of marriage set forth in Vatican II's *Gaudium et Spes:* Marriage is referred to as "the intimate partnership of life and love . . . an intimate union . . . a mutual

giving of two persons" (para. 48). "Married love . . . is an affection between two persons rooted in the will and it embraces the good of the whole person . . . . A love like that, bringing together the human and the divine, leads the partners to free and mutual giving of self, experienced in tenderness and action, and penetrates their whole lives" (para. 49). Here again, the Roman law conception of marriage has been thoroughly imbued with Christian values. This understanding of marriage has important implications not only for marriage jurisprudence within the Roman communion (on which see especially T. Mackin, *What Is Marriage?* [Paulist Press, New York/Ramsey 1982], pp. 283-327 but also for ecumenical relations.

7. P. Noailles and A. Dain, *Les Novelles de Leon VI le Sage* (Paris 1944), 297, trans. L'Huillier, "Novella 89," 158.

8. Noted by L'Huillier, "Novella 89," 160-61.

9. (Paulist Press, New York/Ramsey 1984) 150.

3
The International Theological Commission and Indissolubility

Theodore Mackin, S.J.

The Matthean version of the Synoptic narrative of Jesus' dispute with a group of scribes about the rabbinic tradition permitting husbands to dismiss their wives[1] reports that Jesus' first riposte was to imply that the scribes had asked him the wrong question. They had tried to trap him by asking whose side he took in the debate continuing into their own from the preceding generation. Did he agree with the conservative Shammai, who allowed only the wife's adultery or equivalently delinquent conduct as grounds for dismissal? Or did he side with the liberal Hillel, who allowed dismissal for reasons as trivial as poor cookery: "May a husband dismiss his wife for just any reason?" (Mt. 19:3). In a word, which of the two great teachers did Jesus think interpreted Deuteronomy 24:1 correctly: "When a man, after marrying a woman and having intercourse with her, is later displeased with her because he finds in her something indecent, and therefore he draws up a writ of dismissal and hands it to her, thus dismissing her from his house, . . ."?[2] Was Hillel right in saying that even the husband's displeasure, whatever its cause, is by itself a sufficient ground for dismissal?

Jesus replied by inviting the lawyers to go back to the "beginning," to God's original design for marriage, before Moses attenuated his demand therein in order to accommodate their stubbornness. Marriage is God's invention, not men's. So in every instance it is created and carries on under divine jurisdiction, not human. It is the most precious relationship a man can have: "That is why a man will leave [even] his father and mother and cling to his wife . . ." (Gen. 2:24). The logic implied here proceeds *a minori:* If a man would not think of breaking his relationship with his parents, much less would he do so with his wife.[3]

Moreover a husband and wife are as one person before the people and the law: ". . . and the two of them become one body [or "one flesh"] (Gen.

27

2:24b). So it is absurd to think that a man could dismiss himself—as the author of Ephesians later reasoned by analogy that a cognate attitude would be absurd: "A man never hates his own body . . ." (Eph. 5:29).

From the evidence available to us the earliest Christians suffered no doubts on one point, namely that Jesus' demand for the continuity of a marriage was unexceptionable: "Therefore what God has joined man must not separate" (Mk. 10:9; Mt. 19:6). From the same evidence we know that the other questions lurking in Jesus' use of the Genesis parable were brought into the open only later by inquiring minds under stress. Given that men must not pretend to dissolve what God has joined, is every relationship that men deem marriage really joined by God? Assuming that Jesus commanded reasonably, and that his reason for forbidding the dismissal of wives is that they are "one flesh" with their husbands, in which human gesture are they made so? By the act alone of consenting to marriage? Or is something more needed, something more of the flesh itself? What of the clause in Matthew's record of the dispute that seems to be Jesus' exception to his own interdict of dismissal: "A man who dismisses his wife and marries another is guilty of adultery—except where his wife is guilty of *porneia*" (Mt. 19:9)? What is a wife's *porneia*? Whatever it is, does it exempt her husband from adultery if he dismisses her because of it, and takes another wife?

This serious curiosity ran upon further complication as Christian teachers of the second and third centuries countered pagan accusations by insisting that Christians have sexual intercourse only within marriage, and therein only to have children;[4] and sought to break Gnostic rigorism in their own ranks by arguing that to produce children is a good and holy work. But what if a wife is sterile and thus robs a marriage of its primary reason? May the man who has married her expressly in order to produce children for the kingdom of God dismiss her and try with a second wife? If Jesus' prophetic demand against dismissal holds even in this case, why does it?

Augustine's answer to the second-to-last question here was an unequivocal "no." And it shifted the issue into different territory, the territory into which this essay is a venture. He insisted that not even to produce children for the kingdom of God may a devout Christian husband dismiss his sterile wife and remarry. In fact he cannot do the second because he cannot do the first; he *cannot* remarry because he *cannot* dissolve his marriage. No authority on earth can dissolve it. More than that, it is imperishable; it cannot even die of its own illness.

Augustine addressed this question explicitly in his essay completed in 401, *De bono conjugali* (On the Goodness of Marriage). He insisted at first that not even because of his wife's sterility may the Christian husband in question dismiss her. And he named the reason for the prohibition. It is the *sacramentum* in their Christian marriage: "For in our [Christian] marriages the sanctity of the *sacramentum* is of more value than the fertility of the womb."[5]

That accounts for why a husband *may not* dismiss his sterile wife. Later in the same essay Augustine explained why the same husband *cannot* dissolve his marriage by dismissing his wife. His reason is again their marital *sacramentum*. He uses it to argue by analogy.

> Although that [to produce children] is the sole reason why the marriage took place, even if this for which the marriage took place does not come about, the marriage bond is not loosed except by the death of the spouse. Just as if an ordination of the clergy takes place in order to gather the people, even if the congregation does not gather, there yet remains in those ordained the *sacramentum* of orders. And if because of any fault someone is removed from clerical office, he retains the *sacramentum* of the Lord once it has been imposed.[6]

Augustine argued for the indestructibility of Christian marriages again in his later essay of 418, *De nuptiis et concupiscentia* (On Marriage and Concupiscence), and there used the *sacramentum* in a different but cognate analogy. Having claimed that it is the *sacramentum* that makes the marriage indissoluble, he must show that it itself is imperishable.

> . . .just as the soul of an apostate Christian, in a sense abandoning his marriage with Christ, even though he loses his faith does not lose the *sacramentum* that he received in baptism. Or if he has lost it by apostasy, he would get it back in returning. But he who apostatizes has it to intensify his punishment, not in order to merit his reward.[7]

Augustine set out a more developed version of this analogy in Book II, Chapter 5 of his essay, *De adulterinis conjugiis* (On Adulterous Marriages) of 419. But here he substituted excommunication for apostasy in one facet of the analogy, and the marital bond (*vinculum*) for *sacramentum* in the other facet.

> Even though a person be excommunicated for some crime, the *sacramentum* of baptism remains in him, and will always remain, even though he never be reconciled with God. So too, even though a woman be dismissed because of her infidelity, the bond (*vinculum*) will always remain even though she never be reconciled with her husband. It will end only when her husband dies . . . . [8]

It is typical of Augustine's indecisiveness in these passages that he leaves the reader wondering whether in this one the *sacramentum* and the *vinculum* are identical, or whether the latter is imperishable because reinforced by the imperishable *sacramentum* that accrues in a marriage of two Christians.

A more serious reflection for our purpose is that in this analogy, as in those in *De bono conjugali* and *De nuptiis et concupiscentia*, Augustine does not make the two analogated relationships to be spouse-with-spouse and Christ-with-Church. So he does not in them imply that the Christian spouses are indissolubly bound because the bond of Christ and the Church is indissoluble, and because too the spouses' baptism makes their union an earthly image of the Christ-Church union. This is the heart of the later Scholastic theology of Christian marital indissolubility. But Augustine's analogies are not causal; they are illustrative. There is no *because* in his logic, but only a *just as*. The marital bond *sacramentum* binds the spouses indissolubly *just as* its baptismal *sacramentum* binds the soul to God indissolubly.

That much is a précis of Augustine's case for the indissolubility of marriage, or at least of the marriages of Christian spouses. The intent of this essay is to examine the case that the appointed theologians in the Catholic Church of the last quarter of our own century make for the same doctrine. Because of its adjective the term "appointed theologians" has a specific reference. It designates the members of the Church's International Theological Commission—about whom more in a moment.

But first a qualifying note is in order. To call marital indissolubility Catholic doctrine is not to claim that it has been defined solemnly *ex cathedra*. It has never been the object of such definition. When the Council of Trent declared on the issue in its twenty-fourth session on November 11,

1563, its Canon 7, despite its convoluted formulation, targeted the errant teaching and teachers carefully.

> If anyone says that the Church errs when it teaches, and has taught, in accord with the Gospel and with apostolic teaching, that the bond of marriage cannot be dissolved because of the adultery of one of the spouses; [when it teaches] that the other spouse, even though innocent and having given no cause for the adultery cannot contract another marriage while the guilty spouse still lives; [when it teaches] that a man commits adultery if he remarries after dismissing an adulterous wife, as does a wife who remarries after dismissing an adulterous husband; let him be anathema.[9]

The canon is too nuanced, too qualified by conditions to be a comprehensive statement about marital indissolubility. Nevertheless this indissolubility is common, constant and perennial Catholic doctrine.

What especially raises the examining student's curiosity is the comparison of the Commission's case for indissolubility with that of Augustine, and the contrast of the two cases. Even more interesting, if time allowed, would be to compare with Augustine's the case that held place from the early twelfth century until the eve of the Second Vatican Council. For the Scholastic theologians, and canonists with them, took Augustine's second illustrative analogy above, made it causative, and in the process identified the marital *sacramentum* exactly.

It said that this is found in the Christian spouses' signing forth—in their imaging by their faithful love—the marital love relationship of Christ and the Church. (The most resolute formulation of this identity said that every marriage of two Christians spouses images thus.) This theology made the analogy causative by reasoning that the indestructibility of the divine Christ-Church marital relationship makes the imaging earthly marriage to be also indestructible as long as both spouses live. Implicit in this logic was that the image-to-imaged relationship establishes the causal bridge.[10]

A striking feature of the International Theological Commission's theology of indissolubility that we are about to examine is its near neglect of the same causitive analogy. In face of the momentum of centuries-long use of it by Catholic authorities and theologians the neglect can only be calculated and seriously decided.

About the Commission, it is a kind of subcommittee of the Church's Congregation for the Doctrine of the Faith. In its meeting of December, 1977, the Commission decided to study marriage, its condition and its problems. To this end it created a subcommission of its own. Its members were Carlo Caffarra, Philippe Delhaye, A.L. Descamps, Wilhelm Ernst, Archbishop E. Gagnon, Edouard Hamel, Karl Lehmann, John Mahoney (chairman), Gustave Martelet, Aimé-George Martimort and Otto Semmelroth.

To prepare for its working sessions this subcommission produced five papers (*relationes*) covering each of the following problematic areas: Marriage as institution (written by Wilhelm Ernst), marriage as sacrament (by Karl Lehmann), the relationship of marriage as contract-covenant to marriage as sacrament (by Carlo Caffarra), the indissolubility of marriage (Edouard Hamel), remarriage after dissolution (by Archb. E. Gagnon).

From its discussions of the issues explored in these *relationes* the subcommission formulated a series of propositions, or theses, embodying its conclusions. These were submitted to the entire International Theological Commission for its vote; an absolute majority of the Commission voted in favor of them.

In 1978 Monsignor Delhaye, secretary of the Commission, began publishing the *relationes* in *Espirit et Vie*. All were later published in a single volume titled *Problèmes Doctrinaux du Mariage Chrétien*.[11] With them in this volume were presented the propositions themselves; and to them the subcommittee added a brief commentary on each of the propositions. The commentaries carry the same weight of authority as the propositions in that all were approved by the Commission. They express the mind of every member thereof. The preparatory papers are vouched for only by the author of each.

It goes without saying that a student intending to study seriously the current thinking of the Church on marriage must examine these propositions and their commentaries. To ferret out the theology supporting them he or she must go on and examine theworking papers. It is clear to one who reads both these documents coming from the International Theological Commission and the declarations coming from the Catholic bishops' Synod on the Family of 1980, that at certain significant points the thinking of the former has migrated into that of the latter.

This essay will examine the propositions, commentaries and working papers (*relationes*), not of all five subjects, but mainly of the fourth of these, the indissolubility of marriage. But because the Catholic teaching on indissolubility is grounded mainly in the sacramentality of Christian marriages this essay must examine also the key propositions, and their summaries and papers, concerning the marital sacrament.

Propositions Concerning the Indissolubility of Marriage

Proposition 4.1: The principle.

"The tradition of the early Church, based on the teaching of Christ and the apostles, affirms the indissolubility of marriage, even in cases of adultery. This principle applies despite certain texts that are difficult to interpret and despite examples of indulgence toward persons caught in very difficult situations. The reach and the frequency of this indulgence is difficult to determine."[12]

Proposition 4.2: The teaching of the Church.

"The Council of Trent declared that the Church has not erred when it has taught and still teaches, according to the teaching itself of the Gospel and the Apostles, that the marriage bond cannot be broken by adultery (DB 1807). The council anathematized only those who deny the authority of the Church in this matter . . . . Therefore one cannot say that the council had the intention of defining the indissolubility of marriage solemnly as a truth of faith. However one must take into account what Pius XI wrote in *Casti connubii* in reference to this canon of Trent: 'If the Church has not erred and does not err when it has taught and still teaches this, it is absolutely certain that marriage cannot be dissolved even because of adultery. It is even more evident that the other and much weaker reasons for divorce that are usually adduced have still less validity and merit no consideration.'"[13]

Proposition 4.3: Intrinsic indissolubility.

"Marriage's intrinsic indissolubility can be considered under various aspects and be grounded in various ways. From the point of view of the spouses one will say that the intimate marital union as the reciprocal self-gift of the two persons, the marital love itself, the good of the children—all these demand the indissoluble union of their persons. From this demand there flows the spouses' moral obligation to protect, to maintain and to develop their marital covenant.

"One ought also to put marriage in the perspective of God. The human act by which the spouses reciprocally give and accept one another creates a bond which is grounded in the will of God. It is implied [*est inscrit*] in the creative act itself and transcends human will. It does not depend on the spouses' volition [*pouvoir*] and as such it is intrinsically indissoluble.

"Seen in a Christological perspective the indissolubility of a marriage that is Christian has an ultimate basis that is even more profound. It consists in the fact that a Christian marriage is an image, a sacrament and a witness of the indissoluble union of Christ and the Church. This has been called the *bonum sacramenti*. In this sense indissolubility becomes an experience of grace [*un événement de grace*].

"Societal perspectives too help to ground indissolubility. It is demanded by the institution of marriage itself. The personal decision of the spouses is taken into society, which protects and strengthens it. The ecclesial community especially does this, for the good of the children and for the common good. This is the juridico-ecclesial dimension of marriage.

"All these aspects are closely interwoven. Society itself should protect the fidelity to which the spouses are bound. The Church especially must do this. God the Creator demands this fidelity, as does Christ, who makes it possible by his grace."[14]

Proposition 4.4: Extrinsic indissolubility and the power of the Church over marriages.

"In parallel with its praxis the Church has worked out a doctrine concerning its own power in the domain of marriage. It has set both the extent and the limits of this power. Thus the Church claims no power to dissolve a sacramental marriage that has been consummated. But for very serious reasons—for the good of the faith and for the salvation of souls—other marriages [than those sacramental and consummated] can be dissolved by the competent ecclesiastical authority; or, according to a different interpretation, can be declared dissolved of themselves.

"This teaching is no more than a particular instance of the theory that explains how Christian doctrine has evolved in the Church. Today it is accepted generally by all Catholic theologians.

"However it is by all means possible that the Church could explain more exactly the concepts of sacramentality and of consummation. This would involve explaining their meanings more clearly. In sum, the inclusive doctrine of marriage's indissolubility could be proposed in a more exact and profound synthesis."[15]

The Meaning of the Term "Indissolubility"

A complication one cannot escape in examining the theology of indissolubility is that the meaning itself of the term "marital indissolubility" has changed during the course of Catholic history. Tracing the history is too large a task for this essay. It is enough to examine its complex meaning in current Catholic doctrine and law.

At first sight and apart from the history of this doctrine and law the term "indissolubility" would seem to indicate that marriage in abstract model is a human relationship that cannot end short of the death of at least one of the spouses. But this is not so when the model is realized in actual marriages. In them the word designates their invulnerability to diverse human agents' power to dissolve—their diverse and stratified invulnerability.

Relative to the secular power in civil society the term indicates any and every marriage's invulnerability to this power's will to dissolve. Catholic teaching says that no civil authority has the power to dissolve any marriage, not even the marriages of non-Christians. The ground of this invulnerability to civil authority is not always explained univocally. The uncertainty has to do with the marriages of non-Christians, which are non-sacramental; or if they are sacramental in some way, do not enjoy Christian sacramentality. Is these marriages' indissolubility, i.e., invulnerability, vis-à-vis civil rulers inherent and ontological, in that to dissolve any marriage is simply beyond the civil rulers' power—and therefore this power is forbidden to attempt the impossible? Or could this power dissolve such marriages, but it is unexceptionably forbidden to do so by Christ's prophetic statement, "What God has joined man must not separate"? (Mark 10:9, Matthew 19:6). If the latter is the case, this first stratum of indissolubility is more a restriction set on civil power, but less a trait inherent in real-life marriages. But as we have already seen, the Catholic teaching does point out reasons within marriage why civil authorities' power to dissolve—if in fact it exists—ought never be exercised. These reasons are, for example, the good of children, the good of spouses, the public well-being.

But we are told from another quarter of Catholic teaching and practice that non-sacramental marriages' indissolubility is either not an inherent trait; or if it is, it is "weak" enough to be vulnerable to dissolution by powers other than that in civil society. (To call this indissolubility weak is not off the mark. Catholic law itself, in Canon 1056, says that indissolubility, as an essential trait of marriage taken as a human relationship, gains a special strength in Christian marriage by reason of the sacrament in it. The indissolubility in non-sacramental marriages is thus at least comparatively weak.)

The agencies other than civil authority to whose power to dissolve non-sacramental marriages are, in turn, vulnerable we shall explain later. We note for now only two of these. The Pauline privilege acknowledges a Christian spouse's power to dissolve his or her marriage to a departed unbaptized spouse. This is acknowledged because the marriage was not a Christian sacrament because the departed spouse was not a Christian. And papal power acting in favor of the faith of a Christian spouse dissolves his or her marriage for just cause provided it is not consummated, whether sacrament or not.

About marriages that are Christian sacraments because both spouses are Christian there is the long tradition, dating certainly from the fifth century but perhaps earlier, that these spouses could dissolve their marriages by taking the vows of religious life—provided their marriages were not consummated. Catholic law permitted this until its revision in 1983.

Thus we see others of the strata of indissolubility. A marriage that is a human relationship but not sacramental—which has invulnerable indissolubility against civil power—is yet vulnerable to dissolution by two other powers, that of a Christian spouse's volition, and that of the Roman Pontiff. And a marriage sacramental or not but unconsummated was vulnerable until 1983 to a spouse's pronouncing religious vows; and is still vulnerable to the Pope's power to dissolve. The correlated reasons for vulnerability in these cases are non-sacramentality and non-consummation. Implicit in this Catholic tradition of dissolution is the assumption that Christ's prophetic statement, "What God has joined man must not separate," does not apply to these cases.[16] Or by alternative explanation, at least the papal power to dissolve is not mere human power but is the vicariously held divine power Christ granted to Peter by his words, "What you bind on earth will be bound in heaven; what you loose on earth will be loosed in heaven" (granted to Peter in Matthew 16:19; to an unspecified number of Christ's disciples in Matthew 18:18).

This leaves, by implication, the final stratum of indissolubility. It is the indissolubility of a sacramental marriage (i.e., of two baptized Christians) that has been consummated as a sacrament. Catholic doctrine and law say that no power on earth can dissolve this marriage, not even divine power exercised vicariously by the Roman Pontiff. In one sense this is the least stratum of indissolubility because it contains the fewest marriages. One can guess safely that the consummated sacrament has been and is statistically the least frequent marriage in the human population. But in another sense it is the highest stratum of indissolubility. Not even the religiously most valent power active in the human race can override it. In the Catholic juridical vocabulary this is *radical* indissolubility. There is no doubt that it goes beyond unexceptionable impermissibility. The Pope himself, despite his vicarious divine power, *cannot* dissolve a consummated sacramental marriage.

Is this because of some trait inherent in this marriage? If it is, from what we have already seen it cannot be a trait natural to marriage. Therefore it must be a trait given from outside and above human nature. Whether it is inherent and how it is depends on one's understanding of inherency.

The Power to Dissolve

That approach to the core of this essay was via the meaning of its key term, "indissolubility." A second approach moves via the correlate to indissolubility—its hostile correlate—the power to dissolve marriages. Our first inspection is of the power resident in the wills of the spouses.

These wills are active and decisive in creating the marriage, decisive in that their acts of volition are indispensable. They are the proximate agent. Theirs are the only acts that enter into creating a marriage that is not a Christian sacrament, that is a human relationship and no more.

Where the marriage is of two Christians and therefore presumably sacramental, the spouses' acts of volition are decisive, but they are not the sole causal agents. God is the primary agent. He moves their volition instrumentally in creating their marriage. But he uses their volition in its freedom; he cannot force them to create a sacramental marriage. Rather, he empowers their willing freely to create the sacramental marriage to in fact make it sacramental.

This leads to the question that asks whether in the case of a nonsacramental marriage the spouses' volition can dissolve this marriage (which is distinct from the question whether they can do so with moral rectitude). Catholic tradition apart, and considering only the function of the spouses' volition, it seems that it can dissolve this marriage. For what they do in creating this marriage is to create a relationship, a reciprocal and linking orientation of their persons, a link whose termini are their wills that created the relationship to begin with. There is no reason why the relationship created by and rooted in their wills should be inaccessible to their wills' annihilating it by a counter-decision. (This conclusion too prescinds from the question whether in thus annihilating spouses can act with moral rectitude.)

The Catholic authorities have agreed and still agree with this, as we have already noticed. They once agreed to this *a fortiori* in accepting that two Christian spouses can dissolve even their sacramental marriage, provided it were not consummated, by pronouncing religious vows. One spouse alone could dissolve the marriage by pronouncing these vows. Canon 1119 of the 1917 Code of Canon Law stated this power of the spouses and legitimized its use.

> An unconsummated marriage of baptized spouses, or of one baptized and one unbaptized, is dissolved either in virtue of the law by solemn profession, or by the Holy See's dispensation granted for just cause, whether both spouses request this or one of them . . . .

Canon 1142 of the revised law of 1983 most nearly replicates that old canon. But it omits the clause permitting dissolution by religious vows. It also specifies that papal power dissolves unconsummated marriages not by dispensation but by dissolving them, simply.

> An unconsummated marriage of baptized persons, or of one baptized and one unbaptized, can be dissolved by the Roman Pontiff for just cause, at the request of both parties, or of one of them even if the other is opposed.

Note that the power to dissolve in these cases bears upon a marriage that is sacramental. But to be accessible to dissolution by the two agencies named—the spouses or the Pope—it must be unconsummated.

But even a consummated marriage can be dissolved by a Christian spouse's use of the Pauline privilege. Here the ground of vulnerability to dissolution is that the marriage is not a sacrament because one of the spouses is unbaptized. New Canon 1143.1 states the privilege.

> A marriage entered into by two unbaptized persons is dissolved in favor of the faith of the party who has [subsequently] received baptism, by the fact that a new marriage is contracted by the same party provided the unbaptized party departs.[17]

From the fact that an unconsummated sacramental marriage is vulnerable to a spouse's will to dissolve it (although this vulnerability may no longer be exploited); and from the fact that consummated non-sacramental marriage can be dissolved by papal power or by a spouse's use of the Pauline privilege, it follows by inference that if any kind or quality of marriage is absolutely invulnerable to dissolution it must be a marriage that is both sacramental and consummated. For according to Catholic law this third kind of marriage is the only other kind possible. Indeed, to be finally accurate, this finally invulnerable marriage is not one that is sacramental and consummated, but is consummated as a sacrament. (It is possible that a marriage may be at first consummated while not yet sacramental because one or both spouses are unbaptized, then subsequently be made sacramental when both are baptized, but not consummated since then.)

It is clear by now why one must flex the mind when pondering the Catholic teaching concerning marriage's indissolubility. The first two kinds of marriage—the non-sacramental and the non-consummated—are called indissoluble by this teaching, but can nevertheless be dissolved by the agencies named. Only the third kind, the sacramental marriage consummated as sacramental, is finally, radically indissoluble.

Hence the question: What does the sacramentality of such a marriage do to it to make it invulnerable to the spouses' will to dissolve, and invulnerable to even the supreme authority in the Church's power to dissolve? Or more accurately, what does its consummated sacramentality do to create this invulnerability?

But before we can get at the answer to this question offered by the Congregation's subcommission we must return to the meaning of two more terms in the vocabulary of indissolubility. They are creatures of Catholic law—"intrinsic indissolubility" and "extrinsic indissolubility."

At first reading the difference between them appears to be that intrinsic indissolubility designates invulnerability to dissolution that is a property inherent in marriage; while extrinsic indissolubility designates a limitation set on personal, civil or ecclesiastical power to dissolve. But their meanings are not so simply come by. Both terms bespeak a correlation between a trait or traits in marriages of different qualities and the external powers that might conceivably dissolve them.

Intrinsic indissolubility is the negative correlation between any marriage and civil power. It is the invulnerability of any marriage, "natural" or sacramental, to this power to dissolve. It designates also the invulnerability of a sacramental marriage to the Christian spouses' power to dissolve. Or it designates this at least since 1983 and the exclusion from the revised Catholic law of Christian spouses' power to dissolve their sacramental marriage by pronouncing the vows of religiouslife provided the marriage is unconsumated.

Extrinsic indissolubility designates the invulnerability of a consummated sacramental marriage to any power to dissolve, including that of the Pope.

Thus a reformulation of the question five paragraphs above asks what it is in a consummated sacramental marriage that gains for it extrinsic indissolubility.

The Commentaries on Marital Indissolubility

To do justice to the subcommission's answer to this question in both its formulations, as well as to their answers to our earlier questions, we trace first through the Commentary on Proposition 4 in all its parts, the proposition published by the entire subcommission.[18] It deals specifically with marital indissolubility. We shall afterward examine in finer detail the developed theology of indissolubility in the several *relationes,* the preparatory essays written by individual subcommission members before their meetings. (Their authors alone, not the entire subcommission, vouch for these essays.)

About the Christian Fathers' teaching, the commentary on Proposition 4.1 acknowledges a division of opinion there concerning the permissibility of true dissolution and subsequent remarriage. Lactantius, Tertullian, Origen, the Ambrosiaster, Hilary, Basil permitted both to an innocent spouse, a victim of adultery or of equivalent delinquency in marriage. But the commentary argues that these indulgences were infrequent, unclear in meaning; that the clear and majority opinion of the Fathers sustained indissolubility and the impermissibility of remarriage. (A more accurate judgement on the age is that Catholic doctrine was in the process of formation—with the process heading in the western Church toward an eventual interdiction of the dissolution, for any cause, of at least consummated marriage; while in the eastern Church remarriage was permitted the innocent spouse after true dissolution because of adultery, and later because of other serious delinquencies.) In any case the indissolubility that the commentary claims for that epoch was, in terms familiar to us, intrinsic. By the late fourth century it was an indissolubility that was overridden by the approved Christian practice of dissolution by one or both spouses' entry into a life of vowed chastity.

Paradoxically it was an intrinsic indissolubility whose source was extrinsic to the marriage. Anyone who has read especially the Latin Fathers on the subject knows how rarely they appealed to the sacrament in Christian marriages as the reason against their dissolution (and never appealed to any inherent natural indissolubility); but how persistently they cited as this reason Christ's prophetic utterance, "What God has joined man must not separate." Thus the gripping power of indissolubility in the early Church was obedience to the divine command. It was not a trait, either human or divine, inherent in the marriage. It was not an essential, intrinsic permanence in the marital relationship. It was rather the relationship's resistance, coming from the divine command and from fidelity to it, to the dissolving power of human agencies.

About Proposition 4.1 it is not clear to which species of indissolubility it refers. To which species one can reasonably refer it depends on how one interprets the early Christian tradition. If one finds in I Corinthians 7:12-17, in Paul's instruction to Christian spouses to not hinder an unwilling non-Christian spouse's departure—the source and legitimation of the later dissolution by Pauline privilege—the proposition refers to intrinsic indissolubility. For the theology of this privilege presumes that at least one apostle, Paul, thought that a less than sacramental marriage can be dissolved. And if one accepts the Matthean exceptive clause in the inventory of early Christian tradition, one accepts also that even intrinsic indissolubility does not override the power of a husband to dismiss his wife and remarry without adultery provided he can prove *porneia* against her. And this is a power exercised from within the marriage that overrides its presumed intrinsic indissolubility.

Concerning Proposition 4.3

The commentary on Proposition 4.3 seems, on the face of it, to claim for indissolubility a basis, a source, in marriage the human relationship itself—albeit this basis has needed identification and reinforcement from divine revelation. The basis is that in marriage a man and a woman become one flesh, as one person (Genesis 2:24-25). *Because* a marriage is a profound union of minds, of wills, of love, it is indissoluble.

The commentary continues: "Indissolubility is not something juxtaposed to the spouses' love, not a quality added to it from outside. It is a property itself of the love that is a gift of the self. For the gift of the self, which engages one at the core of the person, transcends any change of mind. It is final [*definitif*]. Sincere love cannot be *ad tempus*. This is why the union it creates is indissoluble."[19]

Just before this paragraph the commentary had said that the decision that creates a marriage is one of those foundational decisions for existence that can be only total and final (there can be no degrees within an absolute). The decision commits a person at that depth whereat he or she disposes of the self totally.

This claims clearly enough that a marriage is in and of itself indissoluble; that indissolubility is one of its essential traits. It claims also—and here, following *Gaudium et spes*, it goes beyond the traditional theology—that the spouses themselves have a volitional, causal role in creating and sustaining the indissolubility of their marriage.[20] The causation is not God's alone, nor the Church's alone. And the spouses' cooperation with God's volition is more than obedience to a divine command.

But all that said, it is still true that indissolubility is not an indestructibility internal to a marriage. Again, it is rather the marriage's invulnerability to dissolution by merely human causes (except, we note again, where human power dissolves it in the Pauline privilege; and where the same power did so in the old practice of dissolving an unconsummated marriage by the vow of chastity in religious life).

It is at this point that the commentary introduces the sacrament and outlines its role in giving Christian marriages their indissolubility. It does not here complete a careful theological examination. That is in the essay Father Hamel wrote in preparation for the subcommission's meeting—which we shall examine presently. What we have here is a commentary on a loose catena of aphorisms.

> Of all the properties of marriage, indissolubility is that which most reveals its sacramental aspect [*bonum sacramenti*]. In Christian tradition the symbolism of the union of Christ and his Church is the basis of the indissolubility of Christian marriages. The gifts of God are unconditional and irrevocable [*sans repentance*]. In the "yes" of God to man in Christ the spouses receive the grace to be as faithful as God himself. Christ says his "yes" to the spouses through their "yes" to one another. In giving themselves to one another they are given by Christ who makes himself guarantor of and the one responsible for their mutual gift. It is he who, at the price of his blood, gives them the strength to love one another to the end.
>
> In the strength of Christ's grace marriage as Law becomes marriage as Gospel. Now the marital bond not only cannot but must not be broken; now the spouses *can* sustain it in fidelity. "You ought" has become "you can."[21]

It seems to me that this inchoate accounting for the role of the sacrament in marital indissolubility changes the subject of the predication. In it indissolubility is not so much the marital bond's invulnerability to any dissolving coming from outside it. It is here the spouses' own ability to sustain their relationship against any attack, whether from outside it or from within themselves. And this ability comes from the sacrament. It follows therefore that the cause of indissolubility is for Christians different from what it is for non-Christians—so different as to be a difference in the nature itself of indissolubility. For the Jew and the pagan it is "Your marital bond must not and cannot be broken by any human agency." For the Christian it is "You can sustain your union against all counter-forces. The reason why you can is that your union is a sacrament. It has been taken up, appropriated by Christ; he has made it an instrument of his own loving will. Since his is valent against all the enemies of faithful love, he makes yours equally valent."

(Here again is this essay's marked-out territory of investigation. In so far as it asks a comprehensive, though multi-faceted question, the essay wants to know 1) the nature of the indissolubility that the sacrament is said to produce in a Christian marriage; 2) how it produces this indissolubility—the dynamics of its causation and the relationship therein, including the role of human volition and its freedom.)

Here in Part 4.3 the commentary becomes sensitive to the last issue named just above. It already sees that if the sacrament locates, perhaps even relocates, indissolubility within the volitionally guided love of the spouses—and because the latter is contingent, is free—indissolubility may be thought contingent in Christian sacramental marriages.

In the rest of this commentary the writer sketches his reply to this *dubium.* Any supposed vulnerability to dissolution is closed off by agents, and by structures too, that are independent of the spouses' volition. They do this closing apparently despite the writer's acknowledging the function of the spouses' free volition in creating the indissolubility fitted to the sacrament.

> Indissolubility is a demand of the marital institution itself. At the level of law it signifies the impossibility of transgressing a norm (validity). In the marriage there is also love and the *communio vitae*, an obligation in justice assumed and protected by society, and transcending the spouses' freedom. At this level one can say that even when love has ceased to exist, the marriage has not. The moral obligation (the bond *must* not be broken) is protected and reinforced by an invalidating law (the bond *cannot* be broken).[22]

The writer seems to say the following: By the agency of the Christian spouses' volition their sacrament brings to their marriage an unassailable indissolubility—thus raising it above the vulnerable indissolubility of the marriages of the unbaptized; but in turn this unassailable indissolubility is saved from any attack coming from the freedom of their Christian volition by a moral obligation in justice native to the non-sacramental marriages of the unbaptized. And this is a moral obligation which creates an ontological indissolubility, one which moves the indissolubility from "ought not be dissolved" to "cannot be dissolved."

But no, he sees the moral obligation coming from a higher, a divine source. And here in his commentary he finally identifies the causes, and the nature itself, of the finally inviolable indissolubility of Christian marriages, of their radical indissolubility.

> For a Christian indissolubility is not pure positive law of God or of the Church. The marriage of two Christians certainly is born of the will of the spouses. It is a personal commitment which invol-

ves a permanent moral obligation of fidelity that is not imposed from outside. But the marriage of two baptized persons is determined still further by the will of Christ. It takes on a supra-personal character that means more than obedience to a command of the Lord. The spouses make their personal commitment at the heart of a sacrament given and received. Christ's will to covenant incarnates itself in the indissoluble sacramental bond that joins the spouses. Thus the indissolubility of a Christian marriage does not lie in the personal commitment alone. It is a profound and mysterious reality, a manifestation of the mystery itself of God. Yet this sacramental *vinculum*—this marriage that is a sign of Christ's covenant with his Church—is expressed in turn in a moral obligation to fidelity. By the agency of Christ's will the spouses are ordered to one another in a permanent reciprocal obligation of dialogue, of pardon and of reconciliation.[23]

Theology of the Marital Sacrament and Indissolubility

These have been the subcommission's brief commentaries on its own Proposition 4 concerning marital indissolubility. They have set forth the reasons—anthropologic, ethical, religious—for indissolubility, but have done so briefly. We turn now to the fuller development of these reasons in the *relationes*, the essays written in preparation for the subcommission's meetings.

Because these reasons are offered in several essays the task of synthesizing them is considerable. I have tried to do so by encapsulating them in quasi-theses—in theses that are developed in theological explications.

One must at the outset note a philosophic difficulty in reading and synthesizing these explications. It derives from their indecisive predication. When they claim conditions and qualities for the husband-wife relationship, they sometimes claim these for "marriage," sometimes for marriages. The former is a claim for the ideal model designed in the mind prior to and free from the real-life experience of marriage. The latter claim is about real-life marriages.

For example, it is one thing to say, with abstract universality, "Christian marriage is a sacrament," since this is to no more than state an element of a model. It is another thing to say, with concrete universality, "Christian marriages are sacraments." This is apparently to assume that all Christian marriages at all times have the traits needed to make them sacraments. We will find the essays at times assuming the latter because of the abstract unassailability of the former. (My own examination will try, with no guarantee of accuracy, to refer to "marriage" where the subcommission theologians do so, but to marriages where they do so.)

*   *   *   *   *

The theologians' first thesis in explaining the sacramentality of Christian marriage is that any and every faithful human love is in itself a sign and an image of God's love for his creation, and is therefore inchoately sacramental.[24] Without claiming historical actuality for the creation poem of Genesis 1 and for the garden parable of Genesis 2 and 3, they see in them a primordial form of God's design for the human race. The design is marital because it is heterosexual and lives under the command to love heterosexually—to leave father and mother and cling together, and to become "two in one flesh." To live and to act this way is what it means for the man and the woman to be in the image and likeness of God.

The theologians' second thesis is a denial of an assumption bred by the Enlightenment thinkers and by the Neo-Scholastic reaction to it in the seventeenth and eighteenth centuries. This assumption is that human beings live in a natural order that is integral, that is not wounded by sin, that contains within itself the possibility of happiness (thus the Enlightenment philosophers and theologians); or that such an order is hypothetically possible, and that the actual order of sin, redemption and grace is this natural order redeemed and graced (thus the Neo-Scholastics).

This thesis insists that God has never intended such an order; that hypothetical or not, it has never existed. Rather, from the first moment of human existence the order has been one of grace and transcendence. Nature itself is a grace, a gift from God; it is the matrix and the beginning of the second gift that is the grace of transcendence. Such an order has multiplied facets of meaning.[25]

All creation is called beyond itself, beyond its own capacity for fulfillment, into union with God. From their beginning human beings have been taken into an order that transcends human capacity left to itself. They have been called to a happiness that surpasses their unaided ability to realize. But they have been graced, they have been given the capacitating gift, to gain this happiness. The substance of this happiness is "divinization," eternal personal union with their creator.[26]

This does not destroy or even demean human nature. It ennobles this nature because it brings it to a superabundant fulfillment of its desires. It frees men and women from sinfulness, illumines their minds about authentic happiness, draws them together in peaceful society, gives meaning and value to the insignificant and humdrum details of life.[27]

To call this also the order of redemption is to say that human malice has crippled it, has infected it with illusion about happiness, with disillusionment and despair about gaining it, and with selfishness and hatred because of these; but that through Christ God the creator has worked and still works to draw men and woman out of this sinfulness—and will do so until the end of history.

This has consequences for marriage. Because any marriage, whether of Christians or others, can be created only by the authentic love of a man and a woman. It is inescapably sacramental because it is evidence of such love in the Creator; and evidence too that the Creator's love is at work in the men and women who live in this way.

This helps to interpret the meaning of Paul's instruction, in I Corinthians 7:39, that Christians should marry "in the Lord." Their marriage cannot be Martin Luther's *weltliches Geschäft,* "a secular affair." For it is taken up, in its nature, into the order of grace. In it nature and grace interpenetrate. And the historical context of this gracing is redemption. This context gives real-life marriages their meaning and character. They belong within God's covenant with the human race to redeem it. Since this covenant has been and is carried out through Christ, all marriages in some way, and Christian marriages most specifically, are created and carry on in Christ.[28]

The third thesis claims that because the only order in history is this one order of grace and redemption through Christ, it is impossible for a person who lives in this order because he or she is Christian, to marry outside it in a "natural," secular, sub-sacramental marriage. In juridical-theological terms, the marital contract-covenant is for this person inseparable from the sacrament. He or she either creates a sacramental marriage or does not marry. Inability or unwillingness to create this marriage leaves him or her not in the fallback alternative of a secular marriage, but in the inability to marry at all.

The Church as Sacrament and the Sacramentality of Marriage

A major thesis in this theology is that the Church exists in an unbreakable love relationship with Christ; that this relationship creates the Church and sustains it in existence. This relationship is also that which constitutes the sacramentality of the Church, since the latter is a visible society, and by this relationship makes Christ's unfailingly faithful love visible in the world.[29] This is also a marital love since it grows in part from the humanity—the male humanity—of Christ.[30] (Note that thus far in the thesis the Church is the ideal model. To say that it exists in an unbreakable love relationship with Christ one must abstract from the reality that it is a society of men and women whose personal and individual love relationships with Christ are contingent on their free decisions, can be destroyed by sinful rejection of him, and are thus not unbreakable. That which is unbreakable, even outside the ideal model and the metaphoric marital relationship implied here, is Christ's love for human beings, his love especially for those who have been brought into a transcendent relationship with him by baptism.)

Ideal model or real society of men and women, the Church is the most accessible means for human intimacy with God, and likewise the richest possibility for loving intimacy within the human race. Christ's resurrection reveals that the Church can bring the world into communion with God. For he is eternally alive as human and is God loving men and women humanly. It is the presence and action of Christ's and the Father's Holy Spirit in men and women, especially in the baptized, that makes this so.[31]

The marital love of Christ and the Church accomplishes perfectly what husband-wife love can only imply and can accomplish only imperfectly. That is, Christ's perfect self-offering does what human spouses cannot do.[32] (Here is one of the infrequent passages in which the Church pictured as abstract model meets the Church in its real-life husbands and wives. It acknowledges, however implicitly, that between the model metaphoric divine marriage and actual marriages there is a gap; and that on the human side of the gap failure is possible and unfulfillment inevitable.)

An effect crucial for this theology of the marital sacrament derives from the blending here of the ideal Church, the metaphoric bride of Christ, with the real-life marriage.[33] Because Christ's relationship with such a Church is marital, a covenant with it of unfailing love, the marriage of two Christians is said to participate in his covenantal marriage. Because, in turn, the Christian spouses' marriage is visible, it is a particular sacrament of the inclusive Church-sacrament. As the bishops of Vatican II said in *Gaudium et spes*, the Christian spouses' marriage is a participation in and an image of the unconditional fidelity of Christ and the Church toward one another.[34]

On this point Karl Lehmann acknowledges that the phrase in Ephesians 5:32, "this is a great mystery," refers not to marriage itself directly. It refers directly to the mystery that is the Christ-Church relationship, namely "the eternal plan of salvation formed by God, that has been realized in history in Christ, and has been made present in the Church." It is into this mystery that Christian marriage is inserted; it is from the Christ-Church relationship that marriage inserted in it gets its full meaning. (The "participation" mentioned just above and the "insertion" claimed here make up a crucial thesis in this theology.)[35]

Baptism and the Sacramentality of Marriage

In their essays the subcommission's theologians dealt for the most part candidly with the question of the "automatic sacramentality" of Christian marriages. In its simplest form this question asks whether, in order that their marriage be sacramental, two Christians need bring no more to their marriage than the fact of their baptism and the perdurance in them of the baptismal character—and that they not have expressly rejected the sacrament. Or is more required of them, some degree of faith and its manifestation; some act of will to make their marriage sacramental?

The theologians' answer begins with the effect that baptism works in a man and woman as a first moment in bringing them eventually to sacramentality in marriage. This effect is accomplished in the Church—in the Church now presented in a second and distinct metaphor, not as the bride of Christ but as his body. This effect is far more than a moral obligation to Christ. To name it in a way that is almost tautological, the effect is to incorporate the person in the body of Christ. Or in the words of Gustave Martlet, it brings about an "ontological insertion" into the body of Christ.[36] (Because the Catholic Church baptizes infants, it follows that their incorporation, their insertion is done apart from any volition of theirs. Since no volition, no free decision is needed in this first step toward marital sacramentality, the question that comes to life and awaits its later answer asks at what point the baptizeds' free decision plays its part in making their marriage sacramental.)

Martelet and Msgr. Delhaye reflect the mind of the subcommission in insisting on the thesis that this volition must have its place. A Christian man's and woman's creating the marital sacrament is not a juridical effect of their baptism. The latter does not merely give them a right to a sacramental marriage, nor does it only qualify them for entry into and occupation of a juridically recognized category of membership in the Church. Far more than that, "their baptism must condition the internal structure of their marriage."[37] They must adhere to their baptism by choice. They must decide freely to "pass through Christ" and let his covenantal love form their own. They must bring their Christian identity into the covenanting. This willed drawing of their incorporation in Christ into their marital sacrament is essential to their creating the sacrament.[38]

The spouses' marital covenant is a further and almost terminal step in completing what their baptism began. The latter incorporated them in the body of Christ, but did so incompletely. The ensuing sacraments—confirmation, Eucharist, penance—carry the incorporation toward completion. Their marriage does the same in its own way.[39]

Christ's Love and Its Effect on Christian Marriages

By his limitless love Christ restored marriage to its original truth. He did this by creating a supreme love union with all of humankind through his life, death and resurrection. His example therein, and his gracing power gained there, now enable men and women to love with the love that God has always intended, with lifelong fidelity. Now in history Christ does this through his Holy Spirit whom he sends into the souls of the spouses.[40]

This he does in and through the visible life of the Church, in the spouses' public commitment to one another there. Thus they attest visibly within the Church that they are united with Christ and that they are drawing on his power to love as he loves. Thus, again, by the power of Christ's Spirit the spouses' love becomes an image of Christ's love for the Church.[41]

Because of their insertion in the body of Christ and because of their gracing there by the Spirit, the baptized spouses' marital relationship enjoys more than an extrinsic analogy to the marital relationship of Christ and the Church. Between these two relationships there is a cause-effect link; the husband-wife relationship exists *because* the Christ-Church relationship exists. It is an actualization in history of the latter, an articulation of it, a participation in it. The Christ-Church *mysterion* is actualized in history in the history of the Christian spouses' relationship.[42]

The Spouses' Volition in Creating the Sacrament

With the theses that the Christian spouses' baptism incorporates them in the Church envisioned as the body of Christ, and that as spouses they actualize Christ's love for his metaphoric body-bride in a real-life relationship, the question concerning the spouses' volition in creating their sacrament becomes more complex. A Scholastic theologian will recognize it as a question about principal cause and instrumental causes—about the relationship between the initiative of the divine principal cause in creating and sustaining the sacramentality of the marriage, and the spouses' role as instrumental causes in this creating and sustaining. What freedom have they in doing so?

The subcommission's theologians made the sometimes neglected point that the spouses are not the only agents active in creating their sacrament, and are indeed not even the principal, finally efficacious agents.

To begin with, the spousal love that lies at the heart of the sacrament, indeed every relationship of persons who seek one another's good, involves a relationship with God, acknowledged or not. He is the condition of every meeting of persons, and its goal. *A fortiori* a love that expresses itself in a total gift of the persons to one another presupposes God's agency.[43] Such a love is possible only in reference to him and in union with him. Without him such unconditional self-giving would bring the human persons to total loss. Only by God's victory over sin secured through Christ's death and resurrection can persons give themselves to one another in full freedom.[44]

This means more than that God has promised the spouses a safe harbor at the end of a life spent in self-giving. Its full meaning is already implied in the thesis that their baptism has inserted the spouses in the body of Christ. Their self-giving love is an instrument and an expression of his own love. And since their love is physical and visible, it is a sacrament of his love.

This speaks to their freedom in creating a sacramental marriage and sustaining it by such a love. Their volition, while in essence free, is nevertheless conditioned antecedently and continually by the will of Christ. To return again to the key thesis here, the spouses' baptisms, by incorporating them in Christ, have joined their wills to his.

> The wills of the spouses do not act simply in their own name and as private persons. Rather they consent as members of Christ's body. By their baptism they are determined intrinsically by Christ. He acts in them and through them.[45]

> The actualization of a sacramental marriage depends entirely on the free will of the spouses. But other realities too condition the quality [sic] of the sacrament. The spouses do not act simply as private persons, but as members of Christ's body, so that in the constitution of marriage they are joined with Christ the head, and with the Church, the body of Christ. These constitutive agents of marriage are linked intimately—even though we have not here analyzed them at depth precisely as thus linked.[46]

In these two statements the serious problem is evident. In the last clause of the second quotation above Lehmann points to it and acknowledges that he has chosen not to probe it. Both the will of God in Christ and the wills of the spouses act to constitute the latter's marital sacrament. Both are free, God's with a divine initiative that alone determines the nature of the sacrament and principally determines its presence in a particular marriage; the human wills with their own freedom, with their function in determining the presence of the sacrament. Thus again the problem in interrogative form: What freedom is left to the spouses in creating and sustaining their sacramental marriage? What do they put in the sacrament that is the effect coming from and correlating to their freedom? Granted for the sake of discussion that two Christians can create only a sacramental marriage, can they exercise their freedom only in deciding to create this marriage and in the consent that creates it? Or does their freedom continue into their marriage? If it does, what can it do there? And to lock the question on the issue of indissolubility, can this freedom destroy the sacrament and dissolve the marriage? If not, why not?

(At this point a cautionary distinction is again in order. Without doubt Christ has forbidden those committed to live in his new covenant to willingly destroy their marriages. But this is not the question of indissolubility. Again, it asks whether this destruction, which is surely forbidden, is within the Christian spouses' power.)

About this matter of the spouses' freedom and its power, Karl Lehmann made a distinction that is a distraction because it is off the point.[47] He distinguished the validity of the marital sacrament from its fruitfulness. He reasoned that the spouses' faith, their right disposition, do not contribute positively to the sacrament's validity. This is produced by Christ; in traditional terms, it is his *opus operatum*, the effect that he produces. He works in the pre-volitional baptismal character of the spouses to do this. If one asks how baptism, despite being present temporally before the act of marital commitment, can function effectively in this act, Lehmann suggested elsewhere that it functions analogously as the recipient's sign-word of faith functions in baptism itself and in a person's contrition in the sacrament of penance. The expression of faith comes in sequence before the baptismal ritual and before the penitential absolution. It is taken into both, and functions in them as the condition for and the instrument of Christ in gracing the neophyte and the penitent.[48]

Lehmann then turned to the theology of the mystical body to validate this thesis at greater depth. Since by baptism a person is "inserted into the body of Christ *ontologically*" [italics mine], he is not the only one to decide the reality and the meaning of his marriage.

He continued that that which the spouses' wills can control is the fruitfulness of their sacrament, i.e., whether in creating it they are graced or not to act in holiness in union with Christ. It is here that the intensity of their faith and their love can dispose them for richer effects of Christ's grace or for lesser. Implicit in the distinction is also the assumption (rich in paradox and perhaps oxymoron) that a person making his or her marriage vows while in serious sin could nevertheless cooperate with Christ to create the marital sacrament. Thus his marital consent would be valid thanks to the efficacious divine action (and because as human agent he does not put the essential obstacle of intending not to create the sacrament); but his consent would be fruitless in grace thanks to his sinful will (in Scholastic terms his making this fruitlessness possible if he consents while in the state of grace is his *opus operantis*).

Lehmann then addressed briefly this difficulty that the distinction makes inescapable. How can a person's sinful will, an otherwise believing Christian's deliberate alienation from God for perhaps years, on the one hand block his gracing but on the other hand not block his cooperation in creating the marital sacrament and sustaining it?

Lehmann acknowledges the commonplace that God's grace in the sacrament does not operate without the spouses' cooperation. It can be made ineffectual by their lack of faith or their lack of love. But he insists that the fundamental claim remains none the less true: In instituting marriage God has, in a way that is irrevocable from his side, promised his grace and joined it to the marriages of baptized Christians. But without doubt one more step must be completed.[49]

> It can happen that in a culpable way such a marriage may be a lie in the function of sign if it includes nothing of what it is supposed to sign as a sign, namely gracious and unifying love.[50]

How then does this "lying" marriage exist as a sacrament? Lehmann's answer is not convincing. It seems to borrow from the thesis we have already seen abundantly, that by their baptism Christians are incorporated in the Church, with the effect that the actions of the Church—of the Church understood as the idealized biblical model—somehow constitute the actions of its members.

> But for the Church considered as a whole, in virtue of Christ's eschatological victory of grace, the link between the sign and signified cannot be broken. Thus the parity of marriage and the Church remains. One can say of the Church what one says of marriage. As a phenomenon visible in history and society the Church is a sign that love is at work and that it conquers in humanity as a whole—God's love for us and our love for God, a love which embraces and unites all men, as long as they do not reject it in a culpable way.[51]

The passage seems to say that a Christian spouse failing at the self-giving love essential for creating and sustaining the sacrament is nevertheless carried along in marital sacramentality because the Church "as a whole," into which his baptism has inserted him, never fails in this love. But what if such a spouse not only fails in this love but rejects it "in a culpable way," as Lehmann admits he may? Is he still carried along in the collective, and apparently idealized, Church-sacrament? Or is he free to disengage from it? And if he is, what becomes of his marriage's sacrament-grounded indissolubility? Lehmann does not probe these questions.

What he does reckon with is the familiar pain that can be brought upon a marriage in the ordinary course of life. He completes the interpretation that is thus far incomplete because it has said no more than that baptism incorporates Christian spouses' marriages in the body of Christ. His completion reminds us that this Christ is the suffering as well as the victorious and triumphant Christ; that his self-giving love that the spouses strive to replicate and prolong led him to final self-donation in death. Therefore insufficient human love need not bring on the marriage's destruction because this love is graced, is carried along, by Christ's love: "The experience of difficulties in marriage are its experience of the suffering Christ. But its human 'yes' is always surpassed by the stronger 'yes' of God."[52]

The explanation leaves untouched the question that asks, as above but in slightly altered form, what is the effect when in the course of the marriage a human "no" clashes with the stronger "yes" of God.

The Sacramentality of Marriage and Indissolubility

The theology we have examined thus far has led to and demanded the question asking about the relationship of Christian sacramentality to indissolubility. It has also gathered and laid in place the elements of an answer to this question.

The subcommission's theologians in fact offer two answers, each approaching the question from a different quarter but converging and becoming one as they arrive at the question. From one quarter they account for the necessity of Christian marriage's indissolubility; from the other they explain the cause of this indissolubility. The first offers a deontological imperative as well as a necessary ontological consequence. Its logic is this: Christ demanded fidelity to God's unconditional will that the spouses' love be an unfailing, lifelong love. He put an absolute demand on the Christian spouses that their marriage imitate and image his own fidelity to his Father's will, a fidelity he realized in his love for the Church.

> What Jesus did in his teaching was to affirm God's unconditional will for unfailing love, for lifelong fidelity.[53]

> To become and remain an authentic image of Christ's love for the Church a Christian marriage must have in it the fidelity that Christ has toward the Church.[54]

This demand, this deontology, elides toward an ontology, a statement of fact about Christian marriages—about their relationship in turn to God's relationship to human beings.

> Two Christian spouses' marriage produces a sacramental effect of God's grace. It participates as a sign, a manifestation of God's gracious commitment to human beings. This *is* an irrevocable commitment and an irrevocable manifestation—and it is always valid.[55]

Surely there is the irrevocable commitment and manifestation, an effect of God's grace. But what specific form of God's grace? And what gracing action produces the irrevocability?

What we found in our examination to this point provides the answer. Because of the spouses' baptism their marital commitment, their unconditional and total self-gift, has been taken into the Christ-Church mystery of redemption. This taking in is the ground of the marriage's sacramentality. The relationship into which it has been taken is the norm, the intrinsic design of the marriage.

> The marriage participates in the manifestation in history of the gracious and unconditional commitment of God, who has established the Church as his fundamental sacrament.[56]

Here participation and incorporation join meaning. Because of them Christ acts continually in the spouses. He it is who brings about the unfailingness, the indissolubility of their union.[57] More than this but building on it, to explain this indissolubility as an effect of the Christian marriage's sacramental character one must see the marriage as incorporated, as inserted most exactly in Christ's unbreakable love commitment to his Church. Because of this the Christian marriage can and does sign forth this unbreakable unity and bring it to reality within itself.[58]

It helps at this juncture to review again what this theology says of the intrinsic indissolubility of marriage—intrinsic in the sense of an essential, inherent property of any marriage. Recalling this will disclose more clearly what the human marital relationship is in itself that is incorporated in the redeeming love relationship of Christ and the Church.

To begin with, in marriage a man and a woman become "one flesh," equivalently one person. Theirs is the most intimate possible union, a sharing of minds, of wills, of love.[59]

A man and a woman create their marriage by one of those basic decisions of existence that can be only total and final, one so absolute as to admit of no degrees. It engages them at that depth at which they dispose of themselves totally.[60]

Indissolubility is not something juxtaposed to the spouses' love, not a quality added to it. It is a property of the authentic love itself which is a gifting of the selves to one another. For this gift of the selves, which engages the spouses at the core of their being, is beyond revocation. It is final.

In Christian tradition the basis of the indissolubility of Christian marriages is their representation of, their symbolizing, their manifesting the union of Christ and the Church. The spouses' commitment to one another participates in God's everlasting commitment to mankind through Christ. In turn Christ's commitment to his Christ-spouse expresses itself in the Christian spouses' commitment to one another. In giving themselves to one another they are given by Christ, who makes himself guarantor of their reciprocal gift and empowers them to love until the end of life.

In words with which we are long familiar, but now interpreting "insertion into the body of Christ" from the side of Christ who appropriates the spouses' marriage, this logic draws its conclusion.

> The marriage of two baptized persons is decided [*déterminé*] by the will of Christ. It gains thereby a supra-personal character . . . . Christ's covenantal love incarnates itself in the indissoluble sacramental bond that links the spouses. Thus the indissolubility of Christian marriages rests not alone on personal commitment. It must be taken as a profound and mysterious, reality, as a manifestation of the mystery itself of God.[61]

Marital Consummation and Indissolubility

Despite this relationship between the Christian marriage and Christ, why in Catholic doctrine is even a Christian marriage thus understood finally indissoluble—why is it invulnerable even to the papal power to dissolve—only if the spouses have consummated it as a sacrament by their first sexual intercourse?

The subcommission's answer to this question is formed from a wedding of the psychology of marital love with the theology of the marital sacrament. The element of psychology is this, that the spouses' self-gift is completed only by their sexual intercourse. Their sharing in love does not reach its human absolute until this intercourse.[62]

The theological element adds that it is this total self-giving in sexual intercourse that Christ has made the full manifestation, the full image of his own mystery, namely his unfailing love for the Church. He has in this way made the husband-wife love irrevocable. And when they engage in this full manifestation, their love and their marriage pass fully into the power of Christ. This is a power that no one, not even the Church in its fullest power, can break.[63]

Despite the seeming absoluteness of this claim, two of the theologians acknowledge contingency at the heart of even sacramental (and presumably consummated) marriages. Fr. Hamel implies a curious distinction between a Christian marriage's indissolubility and its indestructibility.

> . . . marital fidelity finds its most powerful *raison d'être* in the fact that marriage is image, mystery and sacrament of the indissoluble union of Christ and his Church. Thus it is finally the grace of Christ acting at the heart itself of the personal commitment (grace does not create indissolubility but perfects it) which assures the indestructibility of a Christian marriage. The Christian couple is called to form an indissoluble union and to depend on the Lord in order to arrive at it.[64]

Father Martelet acknowledges that even the incorporation of the Christian marriage into Christ's body and the mystery of his redemptive love leaves contingency in the marriage. It does not render its fidelity perfect.

> The insertion of Christian marriage into the body of Christ never eliminates the problem of fidelity for the couple caught in the human condition.[65]

Hence the question, among others, that remains: What does infidelity do to the sacrament? Weaken it because of one or both spouses' sinful denial of love, but never able to destroy it? Or can the infidelity in question also destroy it? (Or—almost an afterthought—how can a marital love commitment taken into the power of Christ ever contradict itself by infidelity?)

Critical Reflections

If I have understood their formally theological enterprise, the subcommission's authors set themselves this task: To verify in Christian marriage a permanence that is invulnerable to either or both spouses' change of mind and reversal of will that could dissolve their marriage. They sought for this verification by reasoning that, in virtue of their marital love and in virtue of their baptism the spouses' own love commitment is "inserted," "incorporated" in Christ and his redeeming love; and the effect of this is that the power of his love makes impossible the dissolution of the marriage by the failure of the spouses' love.

This argument contains an accurate assumption. It is that a marriage cannot end by dying inadvertently. Since the man and woman create their marriage not by a flow of emotion but by an act of volition that is a decision, only a decision can annihilate it. In Catholic tradition it is a decision that ends the marriage in the use of the Pauline privilege and in the now abandoned practice of dissolution by pronouncing the vows of religious life. Even if one were to claim that emotional deterioration and/or affective neglect are the observable causes of a marriage's death, they would cause it as tributary to the volition to end it by letting it die. Hence the theologians are accurate in finding the heart of a marriage's indestructibility in an effect that Christ's volitional love works in the spouses' volitional love.

But it is not clear that in finding marital indissolubility at the juncture of the two wills, divine and human, they have not destroyed freedom in the latter—and thus destroyed the human power to love. When Fr. Lehmann wrote, "These constitutive agents of marriage are linked intimately—even though we have not here analyzed them at depth precisely as thus linked,"[66] he may have hinted that the analysis is incomplete precisely where it ought to have accounted for the survival of this freedom. Fr. Hamel may have intimated the same stopping short when he wrote "Thus the indissolubility of Christian marriages rests not alone on personal commitment. It must be taken as a profound and mysterious reality, as a manifestation of the mystery itself of God."[67] I suggest that the "mysterious reality" is familiar to students of Western theology especially. It is the mystery of human freedom under divine providence.

*   *   *   *   *

I recommend that the words "indissoluble" and "indissolubility" be abandoned. Predicated of sacramental marriages they have suggested for centuries that these marriages hold a quality, an indestructibility, that exists autonomously, that transcends the volition of the spouses. It is to the theologians' credit that they saw how misleading it is to try to sustain this autonomy. They abandoned the centuries-long labor at showing Christian indissolubility's minimal dependence on human volition. They saw the error of confining this volition to the creating of the sacramental marriage and to gaining subsequently the fruitfulness, the grace of the sacrament.

I suggest that to acknowledge the role of human volition we think and speak of "lifelong fidelity" or of "persevering marital love," or of both. From this the theological enterprise will not be to prove the indissolubility of indissoluble marriage in the abstract ideal, but to find out what spouses need in order to live a lifelong marital fidelity, to persevere in marital love to the end. An assumption underlying this suggestion is that such fidelity in love is possible.

But it is a firmly grounded assumption—grounded in the following ways. Marital love has two sources within a person. One is the desire for happiness; it is passion in the classical sense of the word. This is the desire that drives and attracts men and women to one another. The other source is will, the volitional control that can lock this passion onto the beloved person. Sexuality is the bodily expression of these. The locking on can be done freely, by deliberate commitment, by aware self-giving.

Passion and will are the facets of the human psyche in which God's grace can work, in these and in the intelligence. When I speak of his grace working there I use these terms in preference to "giving his grace," because the latter expression suggests a *tertium quid* between God and the human person, something that he passes from himself to the human recipient. To be graced is instead to live and act as moved and drawn by God's moving and attracting action. To be "in the state of grace" is to be of an habitual will to accept and to work with God's moving and attracting.

The heart of this, a reasonable thesis about lifelong fidelity, is that it is possible for men and women to make their passion accessible to God's action so that its strength is intensified and focused. It is possible to those who open their intelligence to his action and thence experience an effect that is crucial to fidelity. This effect is that they are brought to see that no other expenditure of passion, no other commitment of their love is more desirable than the one they have made to create their marriage. In simplest terms, the effect of this gracing of their intelligence is that they cannot make the false judgment that a withdrawal of their marital love or a relocating of it is a greater good than their actual commitment of it in their marriage.

*   *   *   *   *

An especially vulnerable part of the subcommission's theology of indissolubility appears in Fr. Martelet's explanation of the way in which consummation by sexual intercourse finally clinches an indissolubility that is vulnerable to dissolution until that moment. He says that until this intercourse—the first, and it alone suffices according to current doctrine—the spouses' self-gift is incomplete, their sharing in love does not reach its absolute.[68] The converse is his assumption that the first intercourse after the marital vows is the completion of the spouses' self-giving, that in it their love reaches its absolute. Presumable (although this is not in his logic) when this is accomplished their marriage can be taken finally and fully into the power of Christ, which makes it radically indissoluble, invulnerable to dissolution by any other cause than death.

Before asking whether this claim about the first sexual intercourse is true to life in every Christian marriage or in any—whether men and women can reach perfection in love so soon and so easily—one must note that in making this claim Fr. Martelet retreats to a territory of speculation that has been the favorite of Platonic-minded theologians for centuries. This is not the territory where real-life marriages are lived, but the territory of mind and imagination in which ideal models are designed.

This interpretation is in part an inheritance from a juridical determination made by such popes as Gregory IX, Innocent II and Innocent III in the late twelfth and early thirteenth centuries. From the time the Roman and the Germanic traditions of marriage had met and intermingled, they had disagreed about which conduct of the spouses creates their marriage. The Romans insisted that their simple reciprocal expression of consent does so. The Germans insisted that they must do more, must proceed through multiple steps that include, in varied combination, betrothal, exchange of dowry and wedding gifts, expression of consent, entry into the new home, first sexual intercourse. The conflict was resolved by compromise. It was agreed that the marriage is created by the spouses' mutual consent, but that this leaves it still inchoate, incomplete—and vulnerable to dissolution. It is complete, brought to full status—and made indissoluble—by first full sexual intercourse after consent.

In the Germanic mind the two steps came to be the entry into a contract and the subsequent completion of the contract. With a certain logical consistency this helped breed the interpretation that a couple create their marriage by exchanging contractually their right to sexual acts. A further consistency lay in the determination that the contract is completed by the first sexual intercourse, since this is the first use of the contractually exchanged rights.

This was consummation fitted specifically to marriage conceived of as a contractually established legal bond.

In the middle of the twelfth century Pope Alexander III accounted for sexual intercourse's completing the Christian marriage sacramentally. He interpreted Christ's words, "What God has joined man must not separate," to refer only to consummated marriages.[68] As evidence to support this he pointed out that in both Mark's gospel (10:8) and Matthew's (19:6) the clause immediately preceding that one is Jesus' quotation from Genesis 2:24, "That is why a man leaves his father and mother and clings to his wife, and the two of them become one flesh." Alexander completed his logic by saying that Jesus' reason for his command is that husband and wife become one flesh, and that they become one flesh in sexual intercourse.

He supplemented this interpretation by drawing from the image theology that had been used since the Fathers. An unconsummated sacramental marriage is dissoluble because it images only the relationship of Christ with the human soul. But this is a relationship vulnerable to dissolution by the sin of any human being. Therefore the link from model to image cannot produce indestructibility in the latter. But a consummated marriage is indissoluble because it images either the union of the two natures in Christ or the union of Christ with his Church. Both of these are indestructible unions.

Implicit in Alexander's reasoning was the assumption not only that the consummated sacramental marriage ought by moral imperative to be sustained for life because it is an image of an indestructible divine relationship, and to image thus truly it must do so for life. But he implied that being an image of the indestructible divine relationship, the consummated sacramental marriage is *made* indissoluble by this imaging. How a metaphoric marriage of Christ to a metaphorically pictured Church causes indissolubility in real-life marriages he did not explain. His logic can reach no further than to provide consistency to the designing of indissolubility into the ideal model of Christian marriages.

I see no way to get around the fact that in current Catholic law the marital act that it claims consummates the sacrament is intercourse fitted rather to the consummation of a contractually created bond. The resolution of the medieval Roman-Germanic dispute understood consummation as the finishing of something only inchoate, as the completion of something incomplete. Bring this understanding to the consummating of the Christian marital sacrament and a grievous difficulty emerges. What is needed to bring this sacrament—this image of the divine marital relationship of Christ and the Church, this participation in Christ's redemptive love commitment to the world—to completion? No more than a single act of sexual intercourse, usually within twenty-four hours after the wedding? If one is unwilling to believe that but still insists that consummation of the sacrament is the immediate and final cause of indissolubility, one must accept that indissolubility comes to a marriage only after years of tested, patient and persevering love. The only way to keep the doctrine of an early and easy consummation is to go back to treating the sacrament as a juridical category that is incomplete and vulnerable until completed and sealed by a first and single intercourse.

Apparently in his concern to explain how sexual intercourse consummates the sacrament, whether in a single act or in many, Fr. Martelet sought first to explain how it consummates marriage understood in itself, pre-sacramentally. In doing so he offered an understanding of consummation far different from the juridical notion we have just mentioned. He repeated that a man and woman create their marriage by making gifts of themselves to one another. They live their marriage by continuing this self-giving, by sharing in love. But, Martelet insisted, this self-giving is completed in sexual intercourse; their sharing in love reaches its human absolute in intercourse. This enables Christian spouses to consummate their sacramental marriages specifically as sacramental. For it is only the completion and the human absolute of love that can manifest Christ's full self-giving. This imaging of Christ's full and absolutely faithful self-giving is the Christian spouses' consummating of their marital sacrament.

But for which sexual intercourse does Martelet claim this? For an idealized model? For any first intercourse after a Christian wedding? If he means the latter, one must ask if many newlyweds give themselves fully to one another so soon and so easily? If the former, did Martelet presume that the model is brought to reality in any and every first intercourse? Or did he think that years of unselfish expressions of love may eventually become the full self-giving and the humanly absolute expression of love that he requires for consummation of the sacrament? He did not explain. But only if he meant the last is his claim believable.

Not the most trenchant, but also not the most trivial reflection is that Fr. Martelet ought to have worded his conclusion more consistently with the Catholic belief that the power of the Church is that of Christ himself exercised vicariously by his human instruments. One cannot have it both ways. If the power of the Church can dissolve unconsummated sacramental marriages because it is Christ's power exercised vicariously, it is inconsistent to set the power of Christ and that of the Church against one another when explaining why the latter cannot dissolve consummated sacramental marriages. It would have been more accurate to say, as the conclusion, that Christ's power cannot contradict itself.

Further, when Fr. Martelet says that at the moment of consummating intercourse the spouses' relationship is taken fully into the power of Christ, he intends that this intercourse disposes the relationship to be so taken, brings it to a condition to be taken that it had not reached before that moment. He intends this meaning because he says that only in intercourse is the spouses' self-giving love at its fullest, at its human absolute. This is debatable on at least two points. In particular circumstances intercourse may not be a couple's absolute of self-giving love. Patient courage in prolonged illness may supersede it. Secondly, there is again the question whether in real life a single act following so closely after the wedding can produce this fullness. One suspects, again, that Fr. Martelet has here slipped back into the image theology he seems otherwise to avoid.

But I suggest that he has stumbled into inconsistency in yet another quarter. Surely the spouses' self-giving must be wholly free if it is to be self-giving at all. This freedom, if it means anything, means that the self-giving can be later withdrawn. Surely the freedom *ought not* be used to destroy; having made the most serious conceivable love commitment, the spouses *ought not* take it back.

But to account for the indestructibility of the spouses' self-giving love he says that when it is disposed and made ready by intercourse, it is taken into the power of Christ, which is unbreakable. This can mean only that from this moment onward the spouses cannot not love one another with the perfection of self-giving—with at least an habitual perfection of it. Aside from the difficulty of reconciling this with spouses' experience, there is the evident contradiction in this logic. A man's and a woman's love must be free if it is to be love. But when taken over by the power of Christ it loses this freedom. For in explaining (and purportedly proving) indissolubility in this way, Fr. Martelet has also implicitly defined dissolubility as the power, the freedom to withdraw their self-giving love. He has secured indissolubility by denying the spouses this power.

That the issue here is, again, the ancient and familiar one of human freedom in the face of divine grace is suggested clearly by Fr. Hamel in a passage quoted earlier. In the passage he mentioned three elements of the theology of indissolubility. The first is long since familiar and calls for no further comment. The other two are most relevant to the question of the spouses' freedom within indissolubility.

> . . . marital fidelity finds its most powerful *raison d'être* in the fact that marriage is image, mystery and sacrament of the indissoluble union of Christ and his Church. Thus it is finally the grace of Christ acting at the heart itself of the personal commitment (grace does not create indissolubility but perfects it) which assures the indestructibility of a Christian marriage. The Christian couple is called to form an indissoluble union, and to depend on the Lord in order to arrive at it.

I think the second element here is reformulated accurately if instead of the metaphoric "grace of Christ acting at the heart of . . ." one says Christ's gratuitous acting in and with the spouses' love commitment to draw it into union with his own. But Christ cannot do this unless the spouses engage in actual love—which can be self-committing love only if it is free. Fr. Hamel hints at this in saying that grace does not create indissolubility but only perfects it, i.e., that the spouses are already loving one another freely when Christ's love enters it and makes it finally indissoluble. But he does not explain how Christ's doing this leaves the spouses' love free, i.e., leaves it love in fact. Like Fr. Martelet he does not even advert to the need to account for their freedom.

The third element is the statement that both hints at clarity and leaves ambiguity. Given that the Christian couple is *called* to form an indissoluble union, their response to the call must be free or it is not a response. But what is the needed duration of this free response? Momentary, lasting only for the length of the wedding vows? Or a few hours longer, until the love commitment in consummation by intercourse? Or must the response go on for months and even years? If in real-life marriage it must be the latter, the spouses' freedom stays active all that time. And if the response must last a lifetime—which the common experience of temptation to non-love and to infidelity suggests it may—then the freedom lasts a lifetime.

*   *   *   *   *

What the indissolubility of a Christian marriage may be Msgr. Delhaye in his turn hinted when he said that the insertion of a Christian marriage in the body of Christ never eliminates the problem of fidelity for the couple caught in the human condition. Let us suppose that the problem of fidelity he acknowledges here is not that of persevering in marriage and marital love as long as both spouses live, but is the problem of temptation to adultery and resistance to the temptation.

Acknowledging this problem assumes that the spouses could sin seriously, could sin despite their sacrament, despite their incorporation in Christ. In other words, the sacramental incorporation does not take away their freedom to defect by the infidelity of adultery. When one adds to this Fr. Martelet's interpretation of marital consummation, it follows that not even the spouses' perfect self-giving, not even the absolute expression of their love taken under the power of Christ removes this fragility and the freedom it supposes.

If this fidelity in the sense of reservation of love and its sexual expressing to the spouse can be only the product of God's gracious action in Christ helping fragile and always free love to so reserve itself, why is fidelity in the sense of lifelong perseverance not also the product of the same causes? And why does the co-working of these causes not leave the spouses free in the same way that they are left free in the co-working that produces fidelity in the first sense? And if we are to understand marital indissolubility in a way that does not destroy the power to love by destroying its freedom, is this indissolubility not precisely this free and fragile love insofar as it overcomes its fragility in the strength of God's gracious action?

Notes

1. Matthew's version of the encounter is in 19:3-12, Mark's in 10:2-12. Some scholars say that the narrative is an artificial setting for Jesus' prophetic statement on marriage. But authenticity is supported by the character of the confrontation. Some Pharisees approach Jesus to put him to the test—a tactic reported by Mark on six other occasions (3:2-6; 7:1-13; 8:11-13; 11:27-33; 12:13-17; 12:18-27).

2. The Deuteronomic prescription here is not about the permissibility of dismissing a wife, but about that of remarrying her after dismissing her and after she has been taken in marriage by another man. Her first husband is forbidden to remarry her. The prohibition is ritual in nature; the woman has been rendered impure for him by her marriage to the second man.

3. Walter Brueggemann argues that Genesis 2:23a—"This one at last is bone of my bones and flesh of my flesh"—is a covenant formula. He adds, "The covenant formula is further substantiated by the concluding statement of v. 24 . . . The first part of v. 24 has the language of

covenant relations, to abandon (*azav*) and to cleave (*davaq*). The latter term, when used of interpersonal relations, as in any context, is clearly a covenant term." (*Catholic Biblical Quarterly*, Vol. 32.4 (1970) pp. 532-542.

4. Thus, for example, Justin Martyr in his *First Apology*, Chapter 1:29: "Either we marry with only one thought, to have children; or if we forgo marriage, we keep ourselves continent at all times." Athanagoras in his *Supplication for the Christians*, no. 33: ". . . as the farmer, throwing seed into the ground, awaits the harvest, not throwing more upon it, so the procreation of children is the measure of our indulgence in appetite." Minucius Felix in his *Octavius*, 31:5: "With a good heart we cling to the bond of one marriage; in our desire for children we have only one wife or none at all."

5. Chapt. 18, PL 40, Col. 388.

6. Chapt. 24, *op. cit.*, Col. 394. What Augustine thought the *sacramentum* is does not emerge clearly in these passages. It seems not to be the marriage itself, as later Catholic theology will insist it is. It is not the spouses' relationship with one another. Nor is it their relationship's character as an earthly image of the Christ-Church relationship, as the later theology will also understand it. He apparently thought the sacramentum is either each spouse's commitment to God to remain in the marriage until death (*sacramentum* as an oath of fidelity to a sovereign), or is their joint commitment to him. Whatever it is, he thought it something that remains in the soul of each spouse that enjoys the same indestructibility as the *sacramentum* of orders in the soul of an ordained man.

7. Book I, Chapt 10, PL 44, Col. 420.

8. In PL 40, Col. 473.

9. Denzinger-Schönmetzer, *Enchiridion Symbolorum, Definitionum et Declarationum de Rebus Fidei et Morum*, Editio XXXII, no. 1807, pp. 416-417.

10. The Council of Florence said this almost expressly in its decree of union of the Armenian church with the Roman Catholic, in 1439.

> . . . A threefold good of marriage is acknowledged. . . . The third is the indissolubility of marriage deriving from the fact that it images the indissoluble union of Christ and the Church. (In Denzinger-Schönmetzer, *op. cit.*, no. 1327, pp. 336-337)

11. In 1984 Monsignor Richard Malone and Fr. John Connery, S.J. published all these— propositions, commentaries and working papers—in a translation titled *Contemporary Perspectives on Christian Marriage: Propositions and Papers from the International Theological Commission*. Chicago: Loyola University Press.

12. *Problèmes Doctrinaux du Mariage Chrétien*, pp. 100-101.

13. *op. cit.*, p. 104.

14. *op. cit.*, pp. 108-109.

15. *op. cit.*, p. 115.

16. Pope Alexander III used this reason c. 1179 when writing his decision to the bishop of Brescia that a wife who had not had intercourse with her husband could enter religious life and thus dissolve her marriage, because Christ's stricture did not include unconsummated marriages. In a decretal letter in the *Collectio Claustroneoburgensis*, no. 317, he explained that Christ forbade spouses to dissolve their marriages because they become "two in one flesh." But this they do only by sexual intercourse.

17. This repeats the legislation that stated the privilege in old Canon 1120. Note that these canons do not name papal power as the agent of dissolution in this case. As the canons suggest, the first marriage of a person using the Pauline privilege is dissolved by that person's pronouncing the vow that creates the second marriage. Thus it is not only divine power exer-

cised vicariously by the Pope that can dissolve a marriage, but so too can human power exercised by a Christian lay person.

18. In their translation Malone and Connery attributed the commentaries on all the Propositions to Monsignor Philippe Delhaye (cf. their Foreword, p. X).

19. *Problèmes Doctrinaux . . .*, p. 110.

20. The following are the pertinent clauses in the constitution's Part II, Chapter 1, "Fostering the Nobility of Marriage and the Family": " The intimate partemship of married life and love . . . is rooted in the marital covenant of *irrevocable personal consent*" (No. 48, italics mine). "As a reciprocal gift of the two persons this intimate union . . . argues for an unbreakable union of the two" (*ibid.*). The council also reiterated the traditional teaching that its indissolubility is a trait inherent in marriage. But it is a trait of a covenant, not, as had been said for centuries, that of a contract: "Marriage . . . [is of] its very nature an unbreakable covenant between persons . . ." (No. 50).

21. *Problèmes Doctrinaux*, pp. 110-111.

22. *ibid.*, p. 111.

23. *ibid.*, pp. 111-112.

24. Cf W. Ernst, *Institution et Mariage*, p. 166.

25. Thus P. Delhaye, *Note conjointe sur nature et grâce dans la théologie de Vatican II*, p. 311.

26. *op. cit.*, p. 319.

27. *ibid.*, pp. 319-320.

28. Cf. K. Lehmann, *Sacramentalité*, p. 182.

29. In G. Martelet, "Sixteen Christological Theses on the Sacrament of Marriage," Thesis I: "The Sacramentality of Marriage and the Mystery of the Church."

Martelet's essay is not included in the volume, *Problèmes Doctrinaux du Mariage Chrétien*. I have examined it in English translation in Malone's and Connery's *Contemporary Perspectives on Christian Marriage*, pp. 275-283.

30. *ibid.*, pp. 275-276.

31. *ibid.*

32. *ibid.*

33. K. Lehmann, *Sacramentalité*, p. 187.

34. W. Ernst, *Institution . . .*, p. 167.

35. K. Lehmann, *op. cit.*, pp. 183-185.

36. In "Sixteen Theses . . .," Thesis 7: "The Sacramentality of Christian Marriage, Seen by Faith," p. 278.

37. Cf on this point K. Lehmann, *op. cit.*, pp. 201 ff.

38. G. Martelet, "Sixteen Theses . . .," Thesis 9: "Contact and Sacrament," p. 279.

39. K. Lehmann, *Sacramentalité*, p. 200.

40. G. Martelet, "Sixteen Theses . . .," Thesis 6: "Jesus, Renewer of the Original Truth of the Marital Union," p. 277.

41. *ibid.*

42. K. Lehmann, *Sacramentalité*, pp. 183-184.

43. *op. cit.*, p. 186.

44. *ibid.*

45. *op. cit.*, pp. 204-205.

46. *op. cit.*, p. 189.

47. *op. cit.*, pp. 193-194.

48. *op. cit.*, p. 203.

49. *op. cit.*, p. 187.

50. *ibid.*, p. 188.

51. *ibid.*

52. *ibid.*, p. 189.

53. Lehmann, *op. cit.*, p. 181.

54. Martelet, "Sixteen Theses . . .," Thesis 11: "The Indissolubility of Marriage." Note the logical structure here. A condition for a marriage's sacramentality is that the spouses intend lifelong fidelity, and intend it continually. Catholic law draws a conclusion from this thesis, namely that if the Christian spouses intend against this lifelong fidelity they cannot marry at all because the only marriage they can create is a sacramental marriage. Therefore exclusion of this fidelity makes sacramentality impossible.

But we note (for the third time now) that this logic does not touch the question that asks whether if one or both spouses withdraw the commitment to lifelong fidelity after they have once made the commitment and thus created their marriage, the sacrament and therefore the marriage still continue in existence.

55. Lehmann, *op. cit.*, p. 187.

56. *ibid.*

57. *op. cit.*, p. 205.

58. *op. cit.*, p. 186.

59. E. Hamel, *Indissolubilité Intrinsique (Commentaire)*, p. 109.

60. *ibid.*, p. 110.

61. *ibid.*, p. 112.

62. G. Martelet, "Sixteen Theses . . .," Thesis 13: "Why the Church Cannot Dissolve a Marriage That Is *Ratum et Consummatum.*" pp. 281-282.

63. *ibid.*

64. *loc. cit.* p. 112.

65. G. Martelet, *op. cit.*, Thesis 7: "The Sacramentality of Christian Marriage, Seen by Faith," p. 278.

66. In *Sacramentalité*, p. 189.

67. *Indissolubilité*, p. 112.

68. "Sixteen Theses . . .," pp. 281-282.

69. Cf. note 16 above.

4
Sacramentality of Second Marriages

Bernard Cooke

In the previous University of Dayton symposium on Marriage I had suggested that in discussing the sacramentality of Christian marriage it is important to recognize the existential *reality* of Christian married life and the parallel *reality* that some marriages have, at least as experienced human-relationships, ceased to exist. This essay continues within that context of reflection and attempts to examine the extent to which *sacramentality* can attach to marriages between Christians previously married and divorced.

Because the procedure of this essay and the validity of its suggestions depends so much on the theological method used, it would be good to state again the nature of that method. What is distinctive of theological development in the past half century is the awareness that *the* starting-point for theology is the experience of being Christian shared in community by believing baptized persons. Other sources of insight—the Bible, the centuries-long tradition of the Church, theological clarification—need to be used as interpreters of present experience, but it is that experience and the reality it reflects that must remain both context and criterion of authentic theological reflection.

So, in our theological study of Catholic marriage, it is essential that we remain constantly in contact with *what is*. There is no place where the divine saving intent is revealed apart from the lives of humans; it is what happens to people because of God's presence to them that tells us what kind of a God we are dealing with. We have, at least verbally, honored this principle by referring to Christian marriage as a sacrament, and it is important that in our attempts to understand better the nature of Catholic marriage we actively employ this principle.

The term "sacramental" is, like most theological terms, understood somewhat differently by different people, so let me state briefly at the beginning the elements that I see as constitutive of Christian sacramentality and which I will, therefore, be using in my discussion of the sacramentality of marriages between previously married and divorced couples. It seems to me that two things are basic to Christian sacraments: 1) that their meaning interrelates with the meaning of the Christ-mystery and 2) that in terms of *the meaning they communicate* there is a special saving presence of the God revealed in Jesus as the Christ. Needless to say, I do not see such sacramentality as working either automatically or magically; instead, the significance that effects the personal transformation we call "grace" must in each sacramental context be concretely meaningful for the persons involved. Simply put, whatever effect a Christian sacrament has on people, it has in proportion to what it says to them about the saving presence in their lives of the risen Christ, of his Father and of their life-giving Spirit.

If I do not misread him, I think this coincides with what Fr. Ted Mackin said about the sacramentality of Christian marriage in his presentation at our last meeting. Let me quote a few sentences from him, to allow him to speak for himself.

> I suggest that if the theology of the sacrament continues to use the terms *sacrae rei signum*, they be understood to mean that a Christian marriage is a sacrament if its conduct is evidence that God's Spirit is present and active in the relationship. What conduct that may be, I have suggested earlier in this essay. Here I would repeat and insist that God's action in the world, whose intentionality is intimate union of the human creature with himself, is a reconciling and healing action because of the sinfulness of the creature that fears intimacy and its demands. Therefore the marital conduct that is sacramental because evidence of God's action must seek and sustain intimacy and in so doing heal and reconcile—both within itself between the spouses and outwardly from itself in the Christian community and in the human family. (*Commitment to Partnership*, p. 60)

In Christian sacraments—which I would see as extending beyond the liturgical rituals that play an essential role in sacrament—there is a transformation of the meaning of life by the meaning of Jesus' life/death/resurrection and vice versa an interpretation of that Christ mystery by the Christians' experience of life lived in Christian faith. This involves a process of divine/human communication, proclamation of and response to the "word of God," by which the divine presence transforms people's experience and consequently their selfhood. Thus, sacraments "give grace."

When we apply this to Christian marriage we can start with what is now commonly recognized, at least in theological circles, namely that the sacrament is basically the two persons in a distinctive human and faith relationship to one another. The wedding ceremony has its role within the broader context of the sacrament, but it clearly is not the heart of the sacrament. Nor is the sacrament of Christian marriage some abstract institution; it is the concrete social reality of couples whose commitment to intimate sharing of life together bears witness to the mystery of God's transforming love for us humans. In its own down-to-earth way the life of a Christian couple is a profession of faith, an acceptance of the belief that the life and death and resurrection of Jesus make sense, indeed give ultimate sense to the day-by-day happenings—joy and sorrow, life and death, achievement and failure, friendship and responsibilities and hopes and dreams—that make up people's lives.

To the extent that people truly believe in Jesus' Passover to new life, to the extent that they see it as making sense out of their own human experience, this mystery colors their relationships to one another. It can help people to bear together the pain of tragedy. It can put into a richer and more ultimate framework the satisfaction that comes in seeing one's children develop into happy and mature and responsible adults. It can give to human sexuality an eschatalogical finality that situates it firmly in a human personal context. And to the extent that people understand and value their own human experiences they are able to appreciate the humanness that lies at the heart of God's revelation in the human Jesus. So, to the extent that two persons' married relatedness has truly human significance for them and is seen as such by others it provides insight into the significance of Jesus' life and death and new life.

But if this is what sacramentality of Christian marriage is all about, where does the institutional Church's role fit in? In particular, where does ecclesiastical legislation regarding the validity or invalidity of given marriages affect their sacramental effectiveness? I believe the response to this question is far from clear, for it involves the most basic issues that engage us in our present divided Catholic approach to ecclesiology. Perhaps the most fundamental question—and I propose it neither facetiously nor presuming a negative response—is this: can Church officials *by legislation* create reality, or is the structured Church's power limited to providing guidance for Christians in dealing with reality?

Realizing that in our reflection on marriage we are dealing with the *social* aspect of our human existence and that the reality of our social relationships result from our human decisions and the arrangements that implement them, I think we can see an area in which the public recognition given to marriages by the Christian community does provide an element that is basic to sacrament. By accepted convention—and the agencies for establishing such convention can and do change in the course of history—the community acknowledges the existence in a given marriage of those elements which can image God's saving love in Christ—committed self-gift, permanence, fidelity, creativity. Having received such external public accreditation, the marriage can function more effectively in the community as a sacramental sign, as a "word of God."

This takes for granted that the Church's interest in recognizing or not recognizing the "Christian reality" of marriages helps provide for the public orderliness and safeguarding of marriage as a critically important social institution. I do not intend to expand on this, since my topic has to do more specifically with the Christian sacramentality of marriages. However, I believe that it is important to keep in mind that human marriage, even among Catholics, possesses a certain priority to ecclesiastical regulation and even to specific Christian significance, i.e. sacramentality. Traditional Catholic theology has always noted this priority.

Given this priority, I believe we must raise a real and serious question which is a specific instance of the more general question we mentioned a moment ago: can the Church by its official actions make or unmake marriages, or can it at most teach about a reality whose existence depends upon forces other than church law? Granted, the official action of the church can make certain marriages to be *officially approved* marriages—and as already indicated this can have an effect on the recognition given those marriages and therefore on their sacramentality—and it can designate other marriages as "not officially approved"; but does this mean that these latter are not marriages, even Catholic marriages, or only that they are "approved" or "not approved"?

Actually, such questioning could be extended to the whole area of Church teaching about human sexuality and to the misconception in some circles that the Church *legislates* sexual morality for its members. This is a much broader topic, far beyond the intent of this paper—so let us return to the question of the sacramentality of second marriages.

Applying the questions we have just raised to relationships between Catholics who had previously been married and who then after divorce live together in what is generally considered by their society as a marriage, it seems to me that we then must ask: to what extent does the lack of official approval negate the sacramentality of such unions? Repeating what was said above, namely that public community recognition is an element in empowering a given marriage to function sacramentally within the community, we must also recognize that it is not the only element that underpins the sacramental potential of a given marriage. Clearly, the love and devotedness to one another and to their children that a couple manifest by a range of actions, the affective fidelity that marks a couple's relationship over a long period of time despite barriers such as prolonged and debilitating illness, the extension of the marriage's own internal spirit of caring for others in the community—these characteristics of a given marriage speak of the loving and saving presence of God. And they do so of themselves, at least to some extent independently of judgment passed on the relationship by Church officialdom. If two people are living in relationship to one another in truly Christian fashion, no church law can prevent this from being seen and from being "edifying."

If my line of argument has been solid up to this point, it follows that the marriage relationship in question is grace-giving, for sacraments cause grace precisely by being significant. How this intrinsic grace effectiveness functions in a particular instance is, of course, always a matter that depends upon the motives, honesty, etc. of the persons involved—and I grant that in many instances one can be a bit hesitant to characterize people's internal dispositions as thoroughly "Christian." For the moment, however, I would like to suggest that a second marriage context is not *of itself* a "living in sin" for it can be a situation in which God's own Spirit of love is patently, sacramentally, present.

For a few minutes let us look at a hypothetical case, not in order to provide a "solution" to the difficult questions with which we are wrestling, but perhaps to clarify a bit these questions.

Let us suppose that Frank, thirty-three, never married, a deeply believing Catholic, meets and falls in love with Jean. She is thirty, also a deeply devoted Catholic, previously happily married, though childless, to another Catholic for a period of six years. Her husband had become involved, without Jean being aware of it for a long time, with another woman; eventually, to Jean's dismay, he sought a divorce and soon after married the other woman. Needless to say, Jean was shattered by this experience, and her self-esteem only began to be restored when after a lapse of two years she met Frank and discovered and responded to his love for her.

Believing that she had a solid case, Jean applied for an annulment but was refused. At that point she was advised pastorally—rightly or wrongly—that there was no hope of reapplying in another diocese but that her first husband's early infidelity indicated the non-provable but real nullity of that marriage, and that she and Frank have the right to engage in a Christian marriage. So, they are quietly married, move to another part of the country where there is no knowledge of Jean's former marriage and become active members of their Catholic parish . . . to all appearances—and even in their own consciousness—no different from the other Catholic couples who are their friends.

Over the years they are regarded, with good reason, as pillars of the parish; they raise as informed and believing Christians the three children with whom they are blessed; their care for one another and for these children is an example of what a true Catholic marriage can be—in short, they are a loving sacrament in the community to which they belong. And all this they can do with complete sincerity, believing in the advice they had received years before—which means that there is no conscious barrier to the relationship being sacramentally effective between the two of them.

But is their relationship a Catholic sacramental union according to Church law? Without attempting to answer that question, I would ask whether that question is relevant if one is asking about the *sacramentality* of the marriage of Frank and Jean.

Responses to this hypothetical case would certainly be divided, and so it is no surprise that the actual cases of divorced and remarried Catholics raise even more troubling questions. However, it seems clear that in many cases convinced and well-informed Catholics find it difficult to accept the official church judgement that some of their friends who are in a non-officially married situation are not really married and that no Christian sacramentality attaches to their relationship. Or to put it more bluntly—that the relationship between these two divorced and remarried persons is a source of their eternal damnation rather than salvation.

I think one reason why we are engaged in discussions like those in this symposium is the growing awareness that the unmitigated negative judgment of church law does not seem to square with the concrete reality of many such remarriages. Admittedly, other perceptions have motivated us to look more closely at the issue: worry about the injustice inflicted on an innocent party to an earlier divorce, pastoral concern for the "state of the soul" of the two persons in the second marriage, etc.—but I leave such concerns aside for the moment. My only point here is that we are finding it increasingly difficult to argue against the reality, even the Christian reality, of many remarriages of divorced Catholics.

Often when we begin to talk in this way, granting some personal and perhaps religious value to these second marriages, we hedge our judgement by saying that the couple's sincerity and moral goodness and desire to be "reunited" to the church tend to offset the barrier to grace constituted by the marriage itself. Or we say something like "God will somehow accept their attempts to do the best they can, despite their being married outside the Church." Without disputing such attitudes of good will towards the divorced and remarried, I would for the sake of argument suggest that the second marriage itself—i.e. the two persons in their married relationship to one another—is in some cases a source of grace. In other words, the two persons are brought closer to God, become more profoundly Christian and Catholic, because and not in spite of their covenanted relationship of loving intimacy.

For the sake of clarification let me mention again the theological understanding of grace with which I am working at this moment—I understand sanctifying grace to be the radical transforming of a person that takes place under the impact of the saving presence of God. Sanctifying grace is not something that comes to a person, it is the change in a person that results from God being for them.

Put into this context, it seems to me that more than one second marriage manifests the presence of God's sanctifying Spirit, that in some at least of such relationships there is a growth in personal spirituality instead of the diminishing of that spirituality in an earlier marriage, that some at least of such marriages provide for the two people much more of an insight into the God revealed in Jesus' life and death and resurrection than do many "legitimate" Catholic marriages.

I think that most of us have seen cases where a person shattered by a first marriage and divorce where they were victimized, embittered and alienated from their Christian faith in God, have been redeemed as persons because someone entered their life who healed them by loving them and by restoring to them the hope that love, including God's love, is really marked by fidelity. It seems to me that in such cases, the second marriage—not the first marriage—is precisely that which sacramentalizes the indissolubility that we wish to safeguard as a characteristic of truly Christian marriage. Is not the experience of some persons that of seeing the "death" involved in a first marriage failure unexpectedly reversed by a "resurrection" of personal faith and hope through a successful second relationship?

For the moment, I do not know where exactly this leaves us in the practical situation of dealing ecclesiastically with marriages among Catholics. What I think we must say is that there is a body of evidence that we cannot ignore, evidence that does not universally support the institutionalized judgement we have made and still make in cases of Catholics remarrying after divorce. Perhaps we can do nothing more than repeat the statement that we simply leave in God's hands situations that go beyond our human regulations—though to do nothing more than this seems to leave many Catholics in an ecclesial limbo, denying to them, perhaps unjustly, the involvement in a community of faith that is the heritage of the baptized.

(A parenthetical remark seems appropriate at this point: The focus of the Church's official attitude towards divorced and remarried Catholics is the denial to them of Eucharistic communion. Involved in this practical stance is a theological understanding of the Eucharist that needs to be re-examined, an understanding that has continued to be a barrier to Christian ecumenism as well. Fundamentally, the question is one of the necessary "dispositions" for reception of communion, the extent of faith and good conscience demanded for full Eucharistic participation. Without so much as suggesting any position on this issue, I wish only to indicate that the refusal of communion to divorced and remarried persons is a question of Eucharistic theology as much as a question of the theology of Catholic marriage.)

In summary, the basic question I have tried to raise in my remarks is simply this: if our Catholic insistence on the Christian reality and indissolubility of marriages between the baptized is based most radically on the Christian *sacramentality* of marriage, what are we to do with the experienced fact that some second marriages function sacramentally in ways theoretically denied to them by the theology that justifies our institutional arrangements?

5
Remarriage and The Divorce Sayings Attributed to Jesus

Mary Rose D'Angelo

Recent Catholic theology has sought in the Jesus of history a critique and a source of guidance for the church's theologizing, frequently in the expectation that Jesus' mission and teaching will provide either a more liberating and less rigid or a more stable and certain source of faith and practice than the diverse and sometimes ossified history of tradition. But this approach has only enhanced the status of the prohibitions of divorce and remarriage. "Sayings of Jesus" have played a significant role in defending the church's prohibition of remarriage after divorce.[1] This role has actually been reinforced by the use of historical-critical methods for retrieving the teaching of Jesus. Because sayings on divorce and remarriage are "multiply attested," that is, appear not only in Mark but in Paul, and may also have been handed down in Q, a large number of scholars have insisted that the prohibitions of divorce, or of divorce and remarriage, must be counted among a very few sayings that can be traced back to Jesus.[2] This has been taken to imply that they therefore have a special status in church legislation. Seeing the prohibitions of divorce and remarriage as a teaching of the historical Jesus has placed these prohibitions beyond the power of the church to change or modify.[3] They are understood to express "not merely an ideal but a norm" for Christian life.[4]

In recent years, there have been numerous studies of the sayings on divorce and remarriage attributed to Jesus and of issues and texts related to them. Catholic biblical scholars have argued that the early communities that used the sayings and the gospel authors who incorporated them into their narratives felt free to modify and adapt the sayings. The variety of decisions made in these sayings suggests that their collective message may be quite different than the one that is frequently drawn from them. Careful examination of the various versions of the sayings about divorce and remarriage attests to a common context, but to quite different functions of the prohibitions. Thus the sayings themselves show that they mediate not unchanging teaching but rather a series of adaptations and revisions of practice. They demonstrate precisely the communities' prophetic authority to understand, apply, rethink, even suppress the prohibitions in response to their own situations.

This essay will build upon this observation, but will attempt further to change the grounds on which the sayings are discussed by bringing the experience of prophetic authority in the community from the background into the foreground of discussions of these sayings. It will make three major points. The first point will be that by preserving the variety of sayings that were used in the early communities, the New Testament itself manifests the early communities' belief that the authority of the Spirit permitted them to modify and to apply these sayings of the Lord.

Secondly, the essay will call into question the attribution of the prohibitions to the Jesus of history. It is certainly true that prohibitions of either divorce or remarriage appear in at least five different contexts and perhaps three different sources. But multiple attestation shows only their antiquity, not their origin with the historical Jesus. Indeed, the texts themselves offer evidence that the source of the prohibitions may be not the Jesus of history, but the experience of early Christian prophecy. I do not wish to argue that this experience is less authoritative than words of the historical Jesus, but rather to stress its authority in the early community.

Third, I shall argue that the common context in which these sayings occur is the context of early Christian asceticism. In each of the documents in which they are found, they function either to modify or to enforce the demands of sexual asceticism. In their New Testament contexts, the sayings do not express an ideal but rather a variety of expedients; thus they can never provide a really adequate basis for reflection on either marriage or remarriage.

These points can only be made by examining the sayings in very considerable detail. This essay will review the sayings three times, from different perspectives. It will first give a brief description of the sayings and their relation to one another, stressing the variations among the sayings. Next it will review them a second time in order to raise the question of their origin. A third review of the sayings will look at their function in the context of the various works in which they appear, underlining their function in early Christian sexual asceticism.

Sources, Documents and the Variety of Rulings

To alleviate the confusion caused by the complex character of the tradition I shall briefly describe the various occurrences of sayings on divorce and remarriage and the way I understand the relation among these sayings. With a very large portion of my colleagues in the field, I am convinced of the priority of Mark and employ the two or four-source hypothesis to explain the relationship of the gospels of Matthew, Mark and Luke. That is, I believe that Mark was written first and was used by the authors of Matthew and Luke. Matthew and Luke also used a second, lost written source, consisting principally of sayings of Jesus (designated Q), but did not use each other's work. This theory is sometimes elaborated to include written sources for tstrange one for the Pharisees to ask, since the Torah explicitly provides for the special material in Matthew (called M), and one for the special material in Luke (called L). As I have said, a very large proportion of New Testament scholars, especially in the U.S., assume some form of this theory in their work. But a signficant number of others reject it, and would therefore reject the relationship among the sayings that I am about to describe.[5]

If the two-source hypothesis is applied to the origins of the divorce and remarriage saying, there appear to be three sources and possibly four original sayings:

1. Paul (1 Cor. 7:10-11): a command of the Lord that forbids divorce to a woman or to a man, interrupted by a ruling (apparently Paul's) that forbids remarriage to the woman should she divorce.

2. Mark (10:2-9): a saying forbidding polygamy and divorce on the basis of the creation narrative.

3. A second Mark saying (Mark 10:10-12), equating remarriage with adultery.

4. A possible Q saying (Matt. 19:9, 5:32; Luke 16:18), parallel to but verbally different from Mark 10:10-12.

These sayings occur in the writings of the NT in six different versions. A saying from an extracanonical writing of early Christianity, the *Shepherd of Hermas*, should be considered with them.

1 Cor. 7:10-11

> To the married I command, not I, but the Lord, that a woman should not be separated from her husband—but if she is separated, let her remain unmarried or be reconciled to her husband—nor should a man leave his wife.[6]

In 1 Cor. 7:10-11, Paul cites a command of the Lord as forbidding divorce, first to a woman, then to a man. After the ruling to the woman he adds that if she divorces, she must be reconciled or remain alone. It is not clear whether he believes the alternatives of remaining alone or being reconciled to have been a command from the Lord also, nor is it clear that these alternatives apply to a man. In 1 Cor. 7:12-16 Paul addresses the case of a believer (woman or man) married to an unbeliever. In this case Paul uses his own authority to rule that the believer should not divorce, but that if the unbeliever wishes to divorce, the believer is "not bound"—i.e., is free to marry again.[7] Thus Paul clearly believes that he has the right and indeed the obligation to decide in what circumstances the saying of the Lord applies.

Mark 10:2-9

> (10:2) And approaching, the Pharisees were asking him whether it is permitted to a man to divorce his wife, testing him.

> (10:3) But answering he said to them: "what did Moses command you?" (10:4) But they said: "Moses permitted writing a deed of divorce and divorcing."

> (10:5) But Jesus said to them: "For your hardheartedness he wrote this commandment. (10:6) But from the beginning of creation *male and female (God) created them* [Gen. 1:27]; (10:7) *therefore shall a man leave father and mother and cleave to his wife and the two shall be one flesh* [Gen. 2:24]. (10:8) So that they are no longer two but one flesh.

> (10:9) What therefore God has yoked together, let a human being not separate.

Mark 10:1-9 is a debate between the Pharisees and Jesus in which Jesus prohibits divorce. The issue is raised in terms of the man who seeks to divorce, and the question is a strange one for the Pharisees to ask, since the Torah explicitly provides for divorce. Jesus' response opposes the commandment of creation, which is embodied in Gen. 1:27 and 2:24, to

Moses' command to write a deed of divorce (Deut. 24:1). The debate treats Gen. 1:27 as prescriptive, as "what Moses commanded" (Mark 10:3). It is difficult to see Gen 1:27 as a command. Perhaps the command is supplied by combining the verse with a shortened version of Gen. 2:24. This is the case in Matthew's revision of the passage.

Mark 10:10-12

> (10:10) And in the house again, the disciples were asking him about this.

> (10:11) And he said to them, "whoever divorces his wife and marries another commits adultery against her.

> (10:12) And if she having divorced her husband marries another, she commits adultery."

Mark 10:10-12 is a logion given in private teaching to the disciples, who question Jesus about his response to the Pharisees. The format of a private teaching to the disciples following a mysterious or controversial public teaching is a technique of Mark. In these scenes of private teaching Jesus seems to address the Christian hearer/reader directly. When the disciples react with misunderstanding or shock, the reader is invited to a deeper understanding than theirs. Thus it is probable that Mark 10:10-12 originated separately and was placed in this Markan framework. It goes beyond the prohibition of divorce in the public debate (and beyond Paul's rejection of remarriage in the case of the woman in 1 Cor. 7:10) by equating remarriage with adultery. It also differs from the public debate in that the prohibition is both for the man who divorces his wife, and for the wife who divorces her husband. Many scholars have concluded that Mark's version of the saying presupposes a setting in Gentile Christianity, assuming that Judaism did not permit women to initiate divorce. This assumption has been shown to be untrue.[8] What is something of an innovation is that Mark envisions the possibility of a man commiting adultery toward his wife.[9] Legal definitions (whether in Jewish or Roman law) of adultery considered only a wife and her lover as guilty of adultery.[10] The technical definition of adultery sees it as a crime against a husband whose wife is corrupted;[11] it is a threat to the legitimacy of his children. The man's behavior is not completely irrelevant. Were he to accuse his wife of adultery, his behavior would be taken into consideration in the case.[12] But Mark's ruling shows a deep concern with the man's sexual behavior from the viewpoint of sexual purity. Mark does not consider the question of remarriage for a believer who is divorced by someone else.

Matt. 19:3-9

> 19:3 And Pharisees approached him, testing him and saying, "is it permitted for a man to divorce his wife for every cause?"
>
> (19:4) But he answered, "Have you not read that the one who created from the beginning *made them male and female* [Gen. 1:27], (19:5) and said: 'on account of this shall a man leave mother and father and cleave to his wife and the two shall be one flesh' [Gen. 2:24]? (19:6) So that they are no longer two but one flesh. What therefore God has joined together let not a human being separate."
>
> (19:7) They said to him: "Why then did Moses command to give a bill of divorce and divorce?
>
> (19:8) He said to them, "On account of your hardheartedness Moses permitted you to divorce your wives. From the beginning it was not so. (19:9) I say to you that whoever divorces his wife not because of fornication and marries another commits adultery.

Matt. 19:3-8 is a rewriting of Mark 10:2-9; in Matthew, the exchange has been reorganized according to the author's understanding of the form of rabbinic debate.[13] First, the Pharisees are given a question that makes sense in halakic[14] terms; not *whether* a man may divorce, but for what cause. This author devotes special attention to the use of scripture. Matthew completes Gen. 2:24 (although not according to the LXX as we know it) and treats Gen. 2:24 as the commandment and Gen. 1:27 as its explanation: "The one who created in the beginning 'made them male and female' and said, 'For this cause shall a man leave his father and mother and cleave to his wife and the two will become one flesh.'"

Matt. 19:9 is a rewritten version of Mark 10:10-12. Matthew takes over only the portion addressed to the man who divorces. This author transfers it from the format of private teaching to the disciples to the conclusion of the public debate, so that it becomes the climactic point of Jesus' debate with the Pharisees, the full explanation of his use of the scripture. Matthew's version of the saying introduces what has become known as "the exceptive clause." This version does not equate remarriage with adultery absolutely; it excepts the case of "fornication." The meaning of the exception has been debated widely and with much heat;[15] its function will be discussed below. At any rate, the exception seems to allow the man who divorces on these grounds to marry again.

Matt. 19:10-12

> 19:10 The disciples said to him, "If this is the case of a man with his wife, there is no good in marrying."

> (19:11) But he said to them "Not everyone grasps this word, but those to whom it is given.

> (19:12) For there are eunuchs who were born so from the wombs of their mothers, and there are eunuchs who were made eunuchs by human beings, and there are eunuchs who made themselves eunuchs on account of the reign of heaven. Let the one who is able to grasp, grasp.

The use of the format of public/private teaching is less central for Matthew than it is for Mark, but here Matthew provides a new private and shocking teaching for the disciples. In Matt. 19:10-12 the disciples' shock at Jesus' ruling gives Jesus the opportunity to extend the teaching on divorce with a limited endorsement of "eunuchs for God's reign."

Matt. 5:32

> 5:31 "It was said: 'whoever divorces his wife, let him give her a bill of divorce' [Deut. 24:1].

> 5:32 But I say to you that everyone who divorces his wife except for a matter of fornication makes her commit adultery, and whoever marries a divorced woman commits adultery."

Like Matt. 19:3-12, Matt. 5:32 is addressed only to men. It rules that a man who divorces his wife makes her an adulteress, a man who marries a divorced woman commits adultery.[16] This saying uses a legally correct definition of adultery: adultery occurs when a married woman has sex with a man other than her husband, or when a man has sex with a married woman. It can be read either as rewriting Mark 10:10-12 or as incorporating a version of a saying in Q attested by Luke 16:18.

Luke 16:18

> Everyone who divorces his wife and marries another commits adultery, and the one who marries a divorced women commits adultery.

Luke 16:18 is likewise addressed to the man: every man who divorces his wife and marries another commits adultery; every man who marries a divorced woman commits adultery. As in Mark 10:10-12, the divorced man's marriage with another woman is seen as adulterous, but it is not clear that Luke depends on Mark. There are minor verbal correspondences with Matt. 5:32 which make it possible that Matt. 5:32 and Luke 16:18 attest to a saying in Q. Some scholars have claimed that Luke preserves features of the oldest form of the prohibition.[17]

Hermas Mand. 4.1.6

"What then, I said, if the wife remain in this passion?"

"Let him divorce her," he said, "and let the husband remain by himself. But if having divorced her he marries another, he also commits adultery himself."

A final early Christian treatment of the topic is found in a work of the second century called the *Shepherd of Hermas*. In it the shepherd/angelic revealer/lord answers the visionary's questions about leading a pure life. In *Hermas Mand.* 4.1.4-12, Hermas asks what a man should do to avoid pollution if his wife commits adultery. The answer permits, in fact commands divorce, but rules that remarriage would make the man himself an adulterer. Should the wife repent, he is to be reconciled with her. The angel warns that this repentance should be allowed only once; it is not clear whether repetition would leave the husband free to remarry. The same rule seems to apply to a wife whose husband behaves immorally (4.1.8).[18] In fact, the Shepherd forbids living with any one who "practices things similar to the Gentiles," equating such behavior with adultery (4.1.9). The portion of the passage that is closest to the sayings attributed to Jesus in the synoptics and to the Lord in 1 Cor. 7:10-11 is 4.1.6; it is verbally closest to Matt. 19:9. In *Hermas*, there is no reference to sayings of the Lord.

Thus the early Christian rulings on divorce and remarriage exhibit a very considerable variation in the issues which the different versions address and the ways in which the sayings are applied. Paul prohibits divorce on a commandment of the Lord, and requires that a woman who divorces remain unmarried or be reconciled to her husband. On the other hand, he seems to permit a Christian who is divorced by a non-believer to remarry. Mark forbids divorce, and equates remarriage with adultery in the case of the one who divorces, whether man or woman, but makes no ruling about the party who is divorced. Matthew and Luke both rule that the man who divorces commits adultery and the man who marries a divorced woman commits adultery. Matthew also rules that the man who divorces a woman makes her an adulterer. Matthew forbids divorce in all cases except fornication. Hermas requires divorce, or at least separation, in the case of a spouse who commits sexual immorality.

These differences should not be looked upon as trivial, or as apparent only. How then are they to be interpreted? Some might argue that the differences should become the basis of current law or theology. For instance one might argue that because versions in Paul and Mark, the earlier writers, do not forbid a person who has been divorced to remarry, we should permit remarriage to the "innocent party."

But a more thoroughgoing conclusion can and should be drawn from the variations in the commands. Joseph Fitzmyer S.J.[19] and the late George MacRae S.J.[20] both have remarked upon the variety of rulings articulated in early Christianity[21] and have suggested that the lesson that ought to be learned from them is that the church does indeed have the right and even the obligation to reinterpret and reapply the teaching of Jesus. The early communities which used the sayings and the gospel writers who interpreted them in their narratives acted with prophetic authority in appropriating and adapting the sayings. In the words of George MacRae,

> . . . we must discern the process by which the teaching of Jesus was remembered, communicated, interpreted, adapted and enshrined in the practice of the early Christian communities . . . The matrix of modern discernment is, as it was in the churches of Paul and of Matthew, the dwelling of the Holy Spirit among God's people.[22]

In recognizing the variations in the sayings, we already acknowledge that words of Jesus are mediated to us by the prophetic authority of the early communities and the gospel authors. I wish to argue that the prophetic authority of the primitive communities not only lies behind the variations, but also is the source of the prohibitions themselves.

The Question of Origin: Paul and the Risen Lord in the Prophets

This section considers the question of the origins of the prohibitions, ask ing the meaning of their attributions to the Lord in Paul, to Jesus in the synoptics and to the angelic revealer in *Hermas*. It will argue that the original source of the sayings need not have been the Jesus of history. Rather it is possible, and indeed more likely, that the sayings are sayings of the risen Lord speaking in the prophets of the Jesus movement and/or the early Christian mission.

Paul's version is essential to the argument that the prohibitions of divorce originate with Jesus, and it is certainly the case that Paul attributes the command not to divorce to the Lord. But it is far from clear that "the Lord" means to Paul what we mean by the Jesus of history. It is as likely, if not more likely, that when he speaks of "the Lord" he means the risen Lord who is present and speaks continually in the prophets of the early Christian community.[23] A number of texts in 1 Corinthians give evidence of the activity of the spirit in regulating the community life of the churches, and of the church of Corinth in particular.[24] In 1 Cor. 5:1-5, Paul adjures the community to curse the incestuous man, acting with Paul's spirit and the power of the Lord Jesus Christ. Here he authorizes the community to act in the prophetic spiritual power that they share with him.[25] An even more illuminating case is found in 1 Cor. 14:38. There Paul speaks of his regulation of the community worship in 1 Cor. 14:26-33 as a commandment of the Lord.[26] The prophetic character of this commandment is reasonably clear from the context in 14,[27] and Paul announces that if any one has God's Spirit or is a prophet, that person will recognize this commandment as the Lord's (14:37): "If anyone does not acknowledge, that one is not acknowledged (14:38)." Thus it seems that the "commandment" of 14:26-33 proceeds from the spirit of prophecy, in this case from Paul as prophet.[28] Among other legal announcements that have been credited to Paul's prophetic spirit are 1 Cor. 3:17 and 1 Cor. 16:22.[29] These two sayings are not attributed to the Lord.

Paul certainly distinguishes between his own opinions and the command of the Lord; in 1 Cor. 7:12 he makes clear that his counsel to those married to unbelievers is his own, and in 7:25 explains that he has no commandment of the Lord. This care to distinguish his own counsel from dominical commands has sometimes been interpreted as showing that Paul is distinguishing between his own prophetic spirit and the sayings of the historical Jesus. This conclusion implies that the only possible sources of this kind of teaching are Paul's prophetic experiences and the tradition of sayings handed down from Jesus.[30] But this is inadequate; it is more likely that in 1 Cor. 7:12, Paul gives his own resolution of the problem, but claims no prophetic authority for his decision; as in 1 Cor. 7:25, he gives his opinion, while making it clear that it does not have the authority of the Lord's command—or even the authority of a command from Paul himself. 1 Cor. 7:40 is more ambiguous, probably deliberately so; Paul gives his opinion, but reminds the community of his claim to the spirit. 1 Cor. 14:37-38 provides an example of a case in which Paul identifies his own regulation of worship as the command of the Lord; this must imply the activity of Paul's prophetic spirit. But as 1 Corinthians 14 makes clear, Paul is not the only prophet who has spoken to that community. When Paul identifies the prohibition of divorce in 1 Cor. 7:10-11 as a command of the Lord, he may understand it as a word given through another prophet of this community, or a prophet of another community.[31]

Here it is useful to turn to the evidence of the *Shepherd of Hermas*. This second-century apocalypse provides an example of a specialized saying on divorce and remarriage whose origin is unambiguously the spirit of prophecy. In the fourth mandate the visionary responds to the revealer's commands to (sexual) purity by raising the case of a man who discovers his wife in adultery. The response, as I said above, requires him to divorce her lest he become a sharer in her adultery, but also prohibits the man from remarrying, lest he himself become adulterous. Thus the solution in *Hermas* is very similar to the stipulations of Matthew. Yet *Hermas* does not cite the word of Jesus in Matthew. Instead the problem is resolved through the ruling of the revealer. This revealer is a heavenly intermediary (elsewhere called the angel of repentance; cf. *Mand.* 12:6:1) who like the angelic intermediaries of the Apocalypse is unclearly distinguished from the Lord who gives the revelation.[32] He is dressed as a shepherd, is the one to whom Hermas is "handed over" (cf. Rom. 6:17) and is addressed with the ambiguous title "Lord" (*kyrie,* usually translated "sir" in this context). Thus *Hermas* does not use the sayings of the gospels or Paul in regard to divorce and remarriage; it is possible that this author knows neither the written Gospels nor the letters of Paul.[33] But the author does have a command of the Lord to resolve the case he proposes; it is a word given in a prophetic revelation.

What then of the synoptic sayings? At least since Bultmann's *History of the Synoptic Tradition,*[34] it has been recognized that prophetic sayings and regulations ordering the churches' lives have been attributed to Jesus in the gospels.[35] How is it possible that sayings of the early Christian prophets would come to be attributed to the historical Jesus? It is possible because from their origin they were identified as words of the Lord. The early Christian prophets, like those of the Hebrew Bible, probably prefaced their words "in the spirit" with a formula like "thus says the Lord" or "the word of the Lord." There are some Christian examples of a similar though more elaborate formula in the oracles in Revelation 2-3.[36] The Lord who spoke through them was the risen Lord Jesus, who, at least according to Matthew, remains always in the midst of his disciples (Matt. 28:20), is present wherever two or three gather (Matt. 18:18-20).

To see these words attributed to Jesus as words of the Christian prophets, it is necessary to change the way we envisage the context of the gospels and, instead of calling up an image of Jesus beset by the Pharisees, to imagine a community like the one Paul addressed in 1 Corinthians, which included a number of prophets. Indeed Paul urged everyone in that community to seek this gift. We envisage such a community gathering in the spirit, to pray about what to do in some specific case in which a member has divorced and is remarried or wishes to remarry. The answer comes through a word of the Lord in one of the prophets: "The Lord says, 'The one who divorces his wife and marries another commits adultery . . . .'" This word is then remembered in the community as a word of the Lord. Ultimately it comes to the gospel author who, in order to preserve and hand it on, gives it a setting in the narrative of Jesus' career.[37]

This process of handing on the word of the Lord who speaks to the community is easiest to envisage with the sayings in Mark 10:10-12, Matt. 5:32 and Luke 16:18. The equations of remarriage with adultery are articulated in the form of casuistic law, a form which strongly suggests their origin from the risen Lord's regulation of the community. In all three gospels, the saying seems to have been received as an isolated saying and integrated into units that are the work of the three evangelists. Mark presents it as a private teaching for the disciples. In Matthew, it appears as one of the antitheses/interpretations by which the author presents the "righteousness greater than the Pharisees" which Jesus requires of his disciples (Matt. 5:20, 21-48). Luke's even more specialized use of the saying will be discussed below.

The longer, more complex debate in Mark 10:2-9 gives the prohibition of divorce a context in Jesus' ministry, by presenting it in a debate between the Pharisees and Jesus. Can this debate be taken to show that the reference to the Lord in 1 Cor. 7:10 must mean the pre-Easter Jesus? This is by no means the case. Scholars have become increasingly aware that on some level debates between Jesus and the Pharisees reflect the interests and struggles of the early churches face to face with the Judaism of their day.[38]

This debate in particular is fraught with problems of form and of consistency which have been widely discussed. The question the Pharisees are made to ask is best understood as an objection to the established practice of the early church, which the risen Lord defends. Bultmann already regarded the debate of Mark 10:2-9 as a secondary construction.[39] Some scholars have tried to resolve its problems by suggesting that Matthew may have preserved the more primitive form.[40] But this rather desperate expedient involves excepting a number of features of Matthew; it is far simpler to explain why Matthew cleaned up Mark's problematic version.[41] And the form of the climactic saying in Mark 10:6-9 points toward an origin in Christian prophecy. M. Eugene Boring, who has attempted to delineate criteria for discerning prophetic words in the synoptic tradition, suggests that the use of scripture is one characteristic of prophetic sayings. But the use of scripture that he sees as characteristic of the prophets is not an exegetical use, which formally cites and interprets the text, but rather a specifically prophetic use in which "the text is not quoted as a past authority and then commented upon, but is re-presented as the present word of the living *Kyrios* . . . ."[42] Boring's description is an excellent characterization of the differences between the use of Gen. 1:27b and 2:24 in Mark 10:6-8 and its revision in Matt. 19:4-6, where it is prefaced with the question, "Have you not read . . .?" Thus the problems of the debate and the special exegetical character of the central saying taken together show that the setting that Mark gives the prohibition of divorce cannot of itself be taken as evidence that it goes back to Jesus.

When interpreters attempt to describe the teaching of Jesus, the question of whether a saying or stipulation goes back to Jesus must be raised in terms of its function and the setting to which that function is most likely to belong. This question is likely to be raised either in terms of distinctiveness from the early church and from the Judaism of Jesus' time, or, more recently, in terms of harmoniousness with first century Judaism.[43] Thus it is argued by some scholars that the sayings could not have been created by the early church, because they run counter to the practice of Judaism, as well as to Greek and Roman law, all of which provide for divorce and remarriage.[44] But this assumes not only that Jesus' teaching must have been distinctive from his milieu, but that his teaching was the *only* distinctive element in the early church's experience, that the early communities themselves made no contributions to the growth of the tradition that were not merely adoptions of preexisting cultural norms. This is not the case. Rather the early Christian communities adopted norms, including and especially sexual norms, from both Judaism and the imperial world. But they also modified and recreated them in the interests of communal self-definition.[45]

Other scholars, who stress the harmoniousness of Jesus with the Judaism of his time, use two texts from Qumran to confirm the origin of the prohibitions with Jesus. They read these texts as evidence that the Qumran community forbade divorce as well as polygamy.[46] Both of these texts (CD 4:13-5:11, 11 Q Temple 57) express clear rejection of polygamy, but the prohibition of divorce is much less clear.[47] The Damascus Document (CD 4:13-5:11) uses Gen. 1:27b as a prescription of monogamy: "The builders of the wall . . . shall be caught in fornication by taking a second wife during their life, while the instruction of creation is, *Male and female created He them* (Gen. 1:27). Also those who entered the Ark went in two by two."[48] The most striking correspondence is with the Markan debate; both texts seem to view Gen. 1:27 as a commandment regarding sexual practice.[49] This text from the Damascus Document is fraught with problems, and it must be questioned whether it would ever have been read as a prohibition of divorce without Mark 10:2-9, and whether 11 Q Temple 57 would have been read as a prohibition of divorce without the desire to resolve the disputes around CD 4:13-5:11. Indeed, CD 4:13-5:11 could suggest that the nucleus of Mark 10:2-9 originated as a prohibition of polygamy.

As these two arguments of distinctiveness from and harmoniousness with Judaism are usually used, they cancel each other out. But even on their own, they are not decisive. The next step would be to provide a description of the way the prohibitions of divorce and remarriage fit into the ministry of Jesus. Two attempts to do this deserve special mention. Fitzmyer has suggested that Jesus understood his preaching of God's reign in a way not dissimilar from the Qumran community, and that as their rules of purity demanded priestly purity of the entire congregation, the prohibitions of divorce and remarriage are part of Jesus' attempt to make of his movement a priestly congregation continually in a state of ritual purity.[50] A quite different function and context has been envisaged by Elisabeth Schüssler Fiorenza, who has argued that the Markan debate's true purpose is to reject the patriarchal structure of marriage. In her view, Jesus responds to a question about the right guaranteed to men only to dismiss a wife by asserting the original equality of creation as the true basis of marriage.[51] She sets this debate into a reconstruction of the Jesus movement as a renewal movement within Judaism which rejected the patriarchal family.

In her view, Jesus did not seek to extend priestly purity to the entire community, but rather rejected it, seeking to incorporate those who were excluded from the community by the demands of ritual purity.[52]

Schüssler Fiorenza's reconstruction is a rethinking of Gerd Theissen's sociological reconstruction of what he terms early Palestinian Christianity. Theissen provides the insight that Jesus did not primarily found local communities but called into being a movement of wandering charismatics.[53] He divides the sayings about family and sex attributed to Jesus into two categories: more radical sayings which he attributes to the wandering charismatics who were the primary focus of Jesus' mission during his lifetime and who continued his career after the resurrection; sayings like the divorce debate which he attributes to more settled and more conservative local communities in which marriage and possessions played a significant role.[54]

There are a number of points at which questions arise about this picture; for instance, Schüssler Fiorenza has criticized Theissen's assumption that the ascetic wandering prophets were all men.[55] In particular the division into wandering charismatics and settled communities should not be applied in such a way as to exclude prophecy from the settled communities. Such boundaries as are likely to have existed between two such groups must have been extremely fluid. The movement would have included prophetic figures who were "settled" as well as wandering charismatics.[56] In attributing the saying to the concerns of the settled communities, Theissen already suggests that the prohibition of divorce is unlikely to have arisen from Jesus himself. And it is questionable whether the division was a feature of the movement before the death of Jesus. Unlike the gospel of John, the synoptic gospels record only one passover. Thus the time frame from Jesus' appearance as the disciple of John the baptist to the crucifixion may well have been less than a year; the preaching career of Jesus need have been no more than a few months. It is entirely possible for virtually the entire movement to have been literally moving for that amount of time. In this scenario, the question of divorce is unlikely to have arisen during the lifetime of Jesus.

Theissen's theory has implications not only for the history of the divorce and remarriage prohibitions but also for the claim that the sayings of Jesus have unique authority. For it describes charismatic, prophetic activity not just on the part of Jesus but also as a central feature of the life of the community at its very earliest stages. This description implies that other prophets were active during Jesus' lifetime and could have been the source of the tradition. It further increases the difficulty of distinguishing the voice of Jesus during his lifetime from the voice of the risen Lord in the prophets, for it means that the charismatic companions of Jesus would have found it natural to speak in his name almost from the moment of his death. Since they continued the lifestyle of his mission, they would have spoken in and to situations that frequently differed little from those of his ministry. The recognition of the charismatic character of the Jesus movement makes clear that multiple attestation and the high antiquity it presupposes are by no means proof that any specific saying goes back to Jesus himself.

In concluding this part of the discussion, I wish to clarify the intent of my argument in two ways. First, I have not shown (and have not intended to show) that Jesus could not have been the origin of the prohibitions of divorce and remarriage. But I have shown that it can no longer be taken for granted that they originated with Jesus, and have suggested an alternative origin for them in the experience of early Christian prophecy. Second, in arguing that they may derive from the Lord speaking in the prophets rather than from the historical Jesus, I am not simply attempting to call into question the authority of the sayings. I do not necessarily believe that the teaching of Jesus should be regarded as more authoritative than the teaching of the spirit in the church. My concern is to illuminate the experiential context of the sayings. Seeing the sayings as the product of early Christian prophecy gives a new context and I hope new force to a case that has already been made by such scholars as MacRae and Fitzmyer: the case that sees the variety of stipulations as the precedent which authorizes the voice of the spirit in the life of today's Christian communities. This view of the sayings and their variety invites us to abandon attempts to reconstruct a single unequivocal intention of Jesus and ultimately of God that lies behind the differing stipulations. It requires us instead to value the differences, to take seriously the context to which they belong, and look to the prophetic authority in our own communities, asking how these sayings should interact with our context.

Some attempts to ask and answer this question in new ways have suggested that it is appropriate to see them as expressing an ideal of married love, toward which all should aim, but from which, perhaps inevitably, some will fall short. I would suggest that the texts that use these prohibitions do not by any means offer an ideal of married love. Rather their real concern is the tension between the sexual asceticism that swept the early communities and marriage as a guarantee of sexual and social responsibility.

Context: Varieties of Ascesis

This section of the study will examine the relation of the various versions of the sayings to the literary context in which they are now found, and will argue that the sayings are used in all cases in the context of early Christian sexual asceticism, that is, the developing practice of sexual abstinence as a spiritual discipline, especially as an aid to prayer and to spiritual and prophetic experience. The sayings aim first to moderate and then to enforce sexual asceticism.

Once again it seems best to begin with Paul as the earliest of the texts. 1 Cor. 7:10-11 is part of Paul's response to an issue which Paul introduces under the rubric of the Corinthian ascetic slogan "It is good for a man not to touch a woman."[57] Paul accepts and approves the slogan; he introduces modifications of it not because it is too rigorous, or because he prefers another position, but because of "the fornications" (*tas porneias*—sexual lapses). 1 Cor. 7:2-9 is articulated in general terms and prescribes equally for men and women. 1 Cor. 7:10-11, on the other hand, is articulated first and almost entirely in terms of a woman.[58] This contrast may mean that the other stipulations and reflections of 1 Cor. 7:1-24 are all a context for discussing the specific case which the Corinthians have raised with him, the case of a woman who wished to divorce her husband. Given this context, it is probable that she sought the divorce in order to live a celibate life. Paul uses his command and the Lord's to prevent this divorce for the sake of asceticism. In addition, he rules that if the woman should divorce, she should not remarry. It may be that the woman in question was married to an unbeliever, and her case gives rise to the stipulations in 7:12-16. Paul permits divorce where it is sought by the non-believing party in a marriage, and considers the believer not to be bound by the former marriage.[59] Paul issues no prohibition at all of marrying a person who has been divorced. Why then does Paul prohibit remarriage? One answer to this question is the defense of the community's ascetic practice. A divorce for the sake of celibacy which ended in a new marriage would bring the community's asceticism into question—something Paul has already detected or foreseen in his reference to "the fornications" (7:2). This is particularly true in the case of a woman who has sought a divorce. Objections on the part of the first husband, whether a believer or unbeliever, not only would cause dissension within the community, but might also cause them to fall into disrepute and perhaps even danger from their neighbors. In the next century, Justin claims that a persecution was started by a similar situation.[60] A woman who divorced her pagan husband because of her desire not to be tainted by his behavior was accused by him of being a Christian. She appealed to the emperor, asking to "arrange her affairs" and then to defend herself against the charge. Her appeal was granted,[61] but her Christian teacher was prosecuted and found guilty.

Like 1 Cor. 7:10-11, Mark 10:2-12 occurs in a context in which it functions both to moderate and to defend early Christian asceticism. Mark 10:2-16 is an introduction to 10:17-31. In that passage, Jesus publicly counsels the rich man that in addition to keeping the commandments, the one who seeks life must give everything to the poor and follow Jesus. Privately, he promises a hundredfold to the disciples who have left family and possessions to follow him. In Luke's version of the story, the family members who are left include a wife (Luke 18:29-30). It is not necessarily the case that Luke's version is original.[62] Whether or not the author of Mark knew a version of the saying that included wife in the list, the issue must have arisen in Mark's community. Mark 10:2-12 makes clear that the omission of "wife" from the list of family who are left for the gospel is deliberate, that to have "left a wife" for the gospel would be to abrogate the commandment of creation. The relatedness of the two passages is more obvious when it is realized that the words "to leave a wife" (*aphienai gunaika*) can be used to mean divorce (1 Cor. 7:11: *andra gunaika mē aphienai*). Mark 10:13-16 is also intended to lessen or perhaps to direct the impact of Mark 10:28-31. The permission, indeed, the invitation to leave children does not in Mark's view imply the rejection of children from the movement. Perhaps the author understands the invitation to leave children only in terms of the warning in Mark 13:12 that "children will rise up against parents and put them to death."

Thus Mark's public debate seems to function to moderate the call of Christian asceticism. Mark's private teaching, which goes beyond it in equating remarriage with adultery, functions in much the same way as Paul's ruling that if she divorces, the woman ought to remain single or be reconciled to her husband. But it manifests an even greater degree of anxiety about sexual purity than does 1 Cor. 7:1-16.

In Matthew the prohibitions appear in two separate contexts, and in both of these the interest in sexual asceticism and sexual purity is still more intense than in the gospel of Mark.

Matthew's concern with sexual purity as ascesis emerges in the first context in which the prohibitions appear, in the Sermon on the Mount, Matthew's presentation of greater righteousness than that of the Pharisees. In Matt. 5:21-48, Jesus proclaims a series of interpretations of the law that are a way of "being perfect as your heavenly Father is perfect." This search for perfection includes a sexual ascesis in Matt. 5:29-32, where Christian sexual praxis is presented as a "fence" around the commandment, "thou shalt not commit adultery." Verses 30-31 revise Mark 9:43, 47, a sort of exhortation to martyrdom, warning that one cannot prefer eye or hand or foot to the reign of God. Mark's concerns in these warnings are close to those of 1 Maccabees 7 where the seven sons gladly offer their body parts to the torturer in the expectation of the restoring resurrection. They make clear that it is better to let the persecutor take one's hand or eye or foot than to "stumble" and lose eternal life. This concern is preserved in Matt. 18:7-10 which also draws on Mark. Only in Matthew 5:30-31 is the concern sexual; the hand and the eye—"touching" and "looking"—appear as the occasion of sexual sin. In 5:32, Matthew introduces the stipulation of a deed of divorce from Deut. 24:1, apparently treating it as a casuistic law which protects and explains the command against adultery, by assuring that no one can marry a woman who is still another man's wife. Matthew supplants it with a new commandment, which sees any second marriage for a woman as adultery. In this context the exception of the case of fornication is not a permission but a demand to divorce in order to preserve sexual purity. The format in which Matthew places the saying is clearly influenced by Mark 10:2-12; it prepares the reader for Matthew's revision of Mark's debate in Matthew 19:3-9.

As I said above, Matthew's revisions of Mark 10:2-9 essentially seek to make the debate make sense in halakic terms, and it has frequently been suggested that the exception of "fornication" in verse 9 means that Matthew takes the same position on the causes for which one may divorce as the Pharisaic scholar Shammai, an earlier contemporary of Jesus. But even if this is indeed the case, the influence of the rabbinic debate is less important for the interpretation of the passage as it occurs in Matthew than are early Christian concerns with sexual purity. Of recent years there has been an increasing tendency to identify the *porneia* which Matt. 19:9 and 5:32 permit as grounds for divorce with the table of forbidden relations in

Leviticus.[63] This is usually based upon a similarly restricted interpretation of the word where it occurs in the so-called apostolic decree of Acts 15 (see 15:20, 29, 21:25), and upon the use of forbidden relations as an example of fornication in the Damascus Document 5:8-9. But CD 4:13-5:11 also mentions polygamy and sex with a menstruating woman as instances of fornication. *Hermas* uses "fornication" to refer to the wife's adultery: if the husband knows her sin and the wife does not repent, but persists in her fornication (*porneia*) he becomes liable for her sin and the sharer of her adultery (*moicheia*). That Matthew shares this viewpoint is clear; the gospel writer commends Joseph's decision to divorce the mysteriously pregnant Mary privately (Matt. 1:19). But the implications of *porneia* should not be limited to adultery, either.[64] Paul's use of *porneia* in 1 Corinthians gives a good idea of the breadth of this word. He does indeed use it to denote incest (5:1); but he also uses the noun of generalized sexual lapses in 1 Cor. 7:2, and the verb of cult prostitution in 1 Cor. 10:8. In 1 Cor. 6:13-18 he makes visiting prostitutes the prime example of fornication, the illustration that should make the Corinthians understand what is wrong with their tolerance of the incestuous man and their shaky preference for celibacy. This passage serves as an introduction to the commands to be married and stay married in 1 Cor. 7:1-16; marriage is a way of fleeing *porneia* (7:2). For Paul, porneia seems to be the opposite of *enkrateia*, the restraint or self-control that enable him and those like him to be as he is. The use in Matthew should be understood similarly. There is no permission to divorce in the exception for "fornication"; rather the demand for sexual purity outweighs even the commandment of creation.

The new private teaching that Matthew adds in 19:10-12 fully exposes Matthew's own understanding of the character of this demand. The disciples exclaim that in such a case it would be better not to marry and the Jesus of Matthew agrees, offering to those who are able to seize upon it the option of being eunuchs for heaven's reign.

The author of Luke undoubtedly inherited the prohibitions of divorce and remarriage; but this author treats them with very considerable ambivalence. First, in Luke the prohibition of divorce is totally eliminated, even though Luke uses both the preceding and the following passage from Mark.[65] Luke deliberately rejects the prohibition of divorce but retains the prohibition of remarriage. These choices probably reflect the ascetic concerns of this author. For Luke (unlike Mark and Matthew), a wife is among the things that may be left for the gospel (Luke 18:19, 14:26). Marrying a wife is among the things that may be a hindrance to the call (Luke 14:20).

In response to the Sadducees, Luke's Jesus affirms that "those who are made worthy to receive the next world do not marry . . ." (20:34-36).[66]

The prohibition of remarriage probably still holds for Luke, but it appears to be allegorically applied. It is presented as part of a suite of sayings that appear to explain the impossibility of serving God and mammon (16:13). The "moneyloving" Pharisees are made to laugh at this. In response, Luke's Jesus warns them that they are choosing what God regards as abomination, that though the reign of God is being preached, the law does not fail, and that they may not divorce one wife (the law and the prophets) for another (money). He then tells the story of Lazarus and Dives (16:19-31) which drives home the true demand of the law and the prophets, no different than the message of "one risen from the dead" (see esp. 29-31).

Thus Matthew betrays an intensification of interest in sexual purity and Luke rejects the prohibition of divorce for the sake of sexual asceticism. In *Hermas* the concern with sexual purity becomes overwhelming. Here it is clear that the very understanding of family life is focussed upon the sexual purity of Hermas the paterfamilias. In the opening vision Hermas is told by his former mistress Rhoda that he is guilty of lustful thoughts about her, a charge against which he vigorously defends himself. The charge is in fact removed by a second female heavenly visitor, who calls him Hermas the moderate (*enkratēs*). *Mandate* 8 on moderation (*enkrateia*) makes clear that this epithet encompasses more than sexual restraint, but also shows that sexual restraint is its first element. She tells him that God is indeed angry with him, but that his sin consists in a failure to correct his family. A second vision which the seer dates a year later elaborates the charge; the main problem seems to be Hermas' children who are betrayers of parents, engaging in "uncleanesses." The only accusation against his wife is that she does not restrain her tongue. Hermas is to live with her as a sister from then on and she will repent. These opening visions are a particularly significant context for the commands about divorce and remarriage. The shift from Hermas' sexual purity to that of his family appears again. In *Mandate* 4 the Shepherd commands Hermas to maintain purity, refraining from any impure desires (4.1.1-3); it is in response to this command that Hermas raises the question about the husband's responsibility for the wife's adultery. The solution to this question is in a sense the major revelation of this prophetic document (and in particular of *Mandate* 4.1-3), for it endorses a repentance after baptism.

Hermas was written in Rome, and its solution bears an interesting and problematic relation to Roman law; the *lex iulia de adulteriis* (18 B.C.E.) made adultery a criminal charge and stipulated that unless the husband brought charges against the wife he was considered her partner and liable of the accusation of lenocinium—procuring. This legislation shows the continuity of *Hermas'* insistence that a husband divorce an adulterous wife with the sexual mores, or at least the prejudices, of the cultural milieu. But the requirement that the husband remain single in order to take back his wife should she repent is decidedly alien,[67] and indeed extremely risky.[68] *Hermas* is a good example of the dialectic of appropriation and redefinition of cultural norms that is to be found throughout early Christianity.

In all the occurrences of prohibitions of divorce and remarriage in these primitive Christian texts, their context seems to be early Christian sexual asceticism. Paul and Mark exercise the prohibitions in order to moderate the force of early Christian asceticism by rejecting divorces for its sake; both are concerned to protect the ascetic call against practices which would bring it into ill repute. Luke rejects the prohibition of divorce; although the application of the prohibition of remarriage in Luke 16:18 appears to be metaphorical, the ascetic tenor of Luke makes it probable that it was applied literally in Luke's community. Matthew's greater righteousness includes a sexual ascesis that explicitly prohibits divorce in all circumstances except the "fornication" of the wife; implicitly it demands divorce in these cases. The disciples express Matthew's view that these demands are the equivalent of celibacy. *Hermas* demands divorce in the interest of sexual purity if one's wife is discovered in adultery, but prohibits remarriage, in order to allow for the repentance of the divorced wife. The ascetic context of the sayings in these works is of importance to us in two ways. First, it confirms the prophetic origin of the sayings and of their variations; prophetic circles evince a particularly strong interest in sexual purity and asceticism.[69] Second, the context of sexual asceticism and the *ad hoc* character of the sayings themselves mean that they cannot be taken to be a determinative source of reflection and practice about marriage for the church communities of our times. They by no means express an ideal for marriage; rather, they deal with marriage in terms of what is expedient. The ideal toward which ancient Christianity aspired was sexual restraint. Freedom and the spirit were to be found in sexual asceticism.[70]

Thus while I do not believe that the observation that these sayings may come from the experience of early Christian prophecy necessarily undercuts their authority, the context from which they address divorce and even more remarriage does indeed raise profound problems about their use. They do not value remarriage because they cannot not adequately value marriage.

For the most part these texts share the vision of their world that understood marriage as a social responsibility, but personal bondage. They offer freedom by sexual ascesis. But just as marriage in the world from which they come was a patriarchal institution, the freedom through sexual renunciation that the texts envisage was by no means equally available to all. There is a notable contrast between Paul and Mark on the one hand and Matthew and Luke on the other. Paul and Mark see the ascetic demand as addressed to women as well as to men, although it is not clear that women share equally in the ascetic call in the view of either. The Corinthians' ascetic principle is "it is good for a man not to touch a woman." In Matthew and Luke, on the other hand, the behavior of women comes under scrutiny and is of concern to the formulation of the prohibitions. But women are not addressed in these sayings. The discipline that is described in both is addressed to the man. We know that early Christian asceticism as a call to freedom had an extremely strong appeal to women,[71] and the gospel of Luke makes some references to women who practice sexual asceticism. Yet in both Matthew and Luke the demands of sexual asceticism are articulated in an entirely androcentric fashion.[72]

It would be difficult to argue that the church's tradition has overcome the inadequacy of the New Testament as source for a Christian vision of marriage. What is needed is a way of defining sexual mores in terms of relationship and responsibility rather than in terms of purity and pollution. Where will the resources for such a revisioning arise? I suggest that what is needed is a new exercise of the prophetic spirit.

New Prophecies

The rising interest in the role of early Christian prophecy in the formation of the Christian scriptures has prompted scholars to look for elements in contemporary Christian community life that correspond to the functions of prophecy in the ancient churches. Two functions in particular have been singled out for special attention. One is the interpretation of scripture,[73] and the other the service of pastoral instruction in Christian living.[74] The office of pastoral instruction in this regard belongs in a special way to those who can speak with the voice of communal experience, to the tribunals, to organizations like Divorced and Separated Catholics, to the unheard voices of married and single parents, of battered women. This volume is addressed especially to such people, to those who can and must speak to and from these communal experiences; I look forward in hope to the instruction, the upbuilding that you will offer us. But such reflection and instruction is deeply intertwined with communal meditation on the scriptures. So before I close, I wish to point you toward an interpretation of scripture that might inform your task.

Most attempts to use the New Testament as a source for a theological vision of marriage and sexuality follow the lead of Mark 10:2-9 in attempting to base teaching on marriage in the intention of creation expressed in Gen. 1:27. But reaffirmations of creation can never address the history of oppression that is attached to marriage, Christian and otherwise. Instead I would suggest that to re-read, to re-member our communal arrangements of sex and gender in a way that hears and applies God's word to our living communities, we must begin from another use of the scripture in the New Testament. That use is the baptismal tradition of the new creation inherited and passed on by Paul:

> All you who have been baptized into Christ have put on Christ: there is among you neither Jew nor Greek, neither slave nor free, no 'male or female.'

This formula rejects the dispensation of Gen. 1:27 as the basis of Christian life. The unequal sexual arrangements of marriage and social intercourse are no longer appropriate for the communal life. Too often this verse has been cited as an affirmation of primordial or ultimate equality within the community. Gal. 3:28 should not be used as proof that the churches are o.k., that they have at heart the best intentions toward women and the oppressed. Rather Gal. 3:28 must be seen as a call to the future. Remembering it should make and keep us profoundly aware of how badly the churches have behaved toward one member of each of these pairs. It is only very recently that we as members of the churches have begun to take account of the long sinful histories of our communities toward Jews, toward slaves, toward women. This text should not function in our thought as reassurance about our origins, but as a call to massive repentance.

Notes

1. See, e.g., the commentary on canon 1056 in *The Code of Canon Law: A Text and Commentary* (Commissioned by the Canon Law Society of America; ed. James A. Coriden, Thomas J. Green, and Donald E. Heintschel; New York: Paulist, 1985), 742 and n. 11. The Apostolic Exhoration of John Paul II, *Familiaris Consortio*, actually claims that the practice of excommunicating the remarried is based on scripture. See *On the Family* (Washington DC: United States Catholic Conference 1981), 83.

2. See e.g. Pheme Perkins, "Marriage in the New Testament and Its World," *Commitment to Partnership: Explorations of the Theology of Marriage* (ed. William P. Roberts; New York: Paulist, 1987), 5-33, esp. 15-16; also Joseph A. Fitzmyer S.J., "The Matthean Divorce Texts and Some New Palestinian Evidence," *Theological Studies* 37 (1976), 197-226; George MacRae S.J., "New Testament Perspectives on Marriage and Divorce," *Divorce and Remarriage in the Catholic Church* (ed. Lawrence G. Wrenn; New York: Newman Press, 1973), 1-15.

3. These observations are made also by Joseph S. Fitzmyer, "Matthean Divorce Texts," 223-226.

4. Commentary on canon 1056 in *The Code of Canon Law*, 742.

5. See the discussion in Fitzmyer, "Matthean Divorce Tests," 206-207. Two scholars who will be cited in these notes and who are critical of the two-source hypothesis are David Dungan, *The Sayings of Jesus in the Churches of Paul: The Use of the Synoptic Tradition in the Regulation of Early Church Life* (Philadelphia: Fortress, 1971); E.P. Sanders, *Jesus and Judaism* (Philadelphia: Fortress, 1985).

6. This translation is my own, as are those of the texts cited below; I have chosen to represent the differences in the terms used for divorce with regard to the woman and the man. It has been suggested that the difference is due to Jewish legal prescriptions; on this see Dungan, *Sayings of Jesus* 89, n.2. But this is unlikely; the terminology is represented also in Greek and Roman law (ibid.).

7. MacRae, "NT Perspectives," 8-9.

8. Bernadette Brooten, "Konnten Frauen in altem Judentum die Scheidung betrieben? Überlegungen zu Mk 10, 11-12 and 1 Kor 7, 10-11," *Evangelische Theologie* 42 (1982) 65-80; "Zur Debatte über das Scheidungsrecht der jüdischen Frau," *Evangelische Theologie* 43 (1983). 466-78. It should also be noted that the legal freedom of women to repudiate was very considerably limited by pragmatic considerations. See e.g. Aline Rousselle, *Porneia: On Desire and the Body in Antiquity* (tr. Felicia Pheasant; Oxford: Basil Blackwell, 1988), 95.

9. See Rousselle, *Porneia,* 103.

10. Rousselle, *Porneia,* 95-97.

11. See Adolf Berger and Barry Nicholas, "ADULTERY," *Oxford Classical Dictionary* (2nd edition, ed. N.G.L. Hammond and H.H. Scullard; Oxford: Clarendon, 1970), 10-11. In the fifth century it became possible for a woman to divorce her husband for adultery without incurring penalties, though his adultery never became a public crime (as hers would have been).

12. Rousselle, *Porneia,* 79.

13. See Fitzmyer, "Matthean Divorce Texts," 205-207.

14. I.e., in Jewish legal terms.

15. For an account of this literature, see Corrado Marucci, *Le Parole De Gesu' sul divorzio: Ricerche scitturistiche previe ad un ripensamento teological, canonistico e pastorale della dottrina cattolica dell' indissolubilita del matrimonia* (Aloisiana; Pubblicazioni della Pontifica Facolta Teologica dell' Italia meridionale—Sezione "S. Luigi" Napoli; Brescia: Morcelliani, 1973), 333-413, esp. 333-383.

16. Astonishingly, Dungan describes this formulation as "entirely from the woman's point-of-view." *The Sayings of Jesus,* 126.

17. Fitzmeyer, "Matthean Divorce Texts," 200-224.

18. From the mid second century, Justin gives an example of a wife who divorced her husband for immoral behavior, with disastrous results (2 *Apology* 2). The stringent demand made by *Hermas* for separation from sexual immorality was and continued to be the practice of the church throughout Christian antiquity. The essay of John Erikson in this volume shows that it was continued by the Orthodox Church.

19. "Matthean Divorce Texts," 224.

20. "NT Perspectives," 9-10, 12.

21. It should be noted that Fitzmyer and MacRae see, or at least focus upon, fewer variations than I have described. They focus upon 1 Cor. 7:12-16 and the exceptive clause in Matthew.

22. "NT Perspectives," 12.

23. On Christian prophets speaking in the name of Jesus as Lord, see M. Eugene Boring, "How May We Identify Oracles of Christian Prophets in the Synoptic Tradition? Mark 3:28-29 as a Test Case," *JBL* 91 (1972), 501-521, esp. 502.

24. On prophets and moral teaching, see David Hill, "Christian Prophets as Teachers or Instructors in the Church," *Prophetic Vocation in the New Testament and Today* (ed. Johannes Panagopoulos; Supplements to Novum Testamentum 45; Leiden: E.J. Brill, 1977), 108-130. This treatment downplays the ecstatic character of the prophetic function, I think excessively.

25. On 1 Cor. 5:1-5 as revealing the context of early Christian prophecy see J. Reiling, "Prophecy, the Spirit and the Church," *Prophetic Vocation* (ed. J. Panagopoulos) 58-76, esp. 60-66. See also Ernst Kasemann, "Sentences of Holy Law in the New Testament," *New Testament Qeustions of Today* (London: SCM, 1969), 66- 81, esp. 70-74.

26. If 14:34-35 is regarded as genuine rather than an interpolation, then silencing of women in the assembly also falls under the rubric of the commandment. However I regard this as unlikely in the extreme, primarily on the basis of the conflict with 1 Cor. 11:6-7. For a presentation of this case, see H. Conzelmann, *1 Corinthians* (tr. J. W. Leitch; Hermeneia; Philadelphia: Fortress), 1975, 246, n. 53-57. Unlike Conzelmann, I see the textual evidence as signficant. For an attempt to reconcile the passage with 1 Cor. 11:4-7, see Elisabeth Schüssler Fiorenza, *In Memory of Her: A Feminist Theological Reconstruction of Christain Origins* (New York: Crossroad, 1983), 232-233.

27. Boring regards 1 Corinthians 14 as the only discussin of early Christain prophecy from the period before the fixing of the Jesus tradition in the gospels ("Christians Prophets," 504-505).

28. Käsemann, "Sentences of Holy Law," 67-69, 74. Although the form of 14:38 is of extreme importance to Käsemann's argument, he also sees the earlier stipulations of 14 as falling under its sanction.

29. Käsemann, "Sentences of Holy Law," 66-68, 69.

30. David Dungan, following Moffat, concludes on the grounds of this distinction that Paul must be attributing the saying to the pre-resurrection Jesus. But this is by no means necessarily the case. *The Sayings of Jesus,* 101.

31. Boring ("Christian Prophets," 5-5-505) suggests that Paul and other prophets may have used traditional sayings, but have delivered them as a word of the risen Lord in their own present.

32. Note the way the angel of Rev. 22:6-20 finally appears to speak with the voice of Jesus.

33. On date of *Hermas* see the *Oxford Dictionary of the Christian Church* (ed. F.L. Cross and E.A. Livinston; 2nd Edition; Oxford: Oxford University Press, 1974) 640-641; introduction in Kirsopp Lake, *The Apostolic Fathers* II (LCL; Cambridge, MA: Harvard University Press, 1917), 2-3.

34. First published as *Geschichte der synoptischen Tradition* in 1921; English translation of enlarged and revised edition published in 1963 by Basil Blackwell, Oxford.

35. For the literature, see Boring, "Christian Prophets" 501-502, nn. 1-2. Note that Bultmann was not the first to suggest this.

36. E.G. Rev. 2:1: "Thus says the one who holds the seven stars in his hand, who walks in the middle of the seven lampstands . . . ."

37. See the similar but briefer description in Howard Teeple, "The Oral Tradition That Never Existed," *JBL* 89 (1970), 57.

38. On the question of the role of the Pharisees see the survey in E.P. Sanders, *Jesus and Judaism* (Philadephia: Fortress, 1985) 291-292. Note that the question is most trenchantly put (as is so often the case) by Morton Smith; see *Jesus the Magician* (New York, 1978), 153-157.

39. *History of the Synoptic Tradition,* 26-27, 385-386.

40. E.g. Dungan, *The Sayings of Jesus,* 1-2-1-7; Sanders (*Jesus and Judaism,* 256-260) discusses the passage without resolving literary priority.

41. See MacRae, "NT Perspectives," 4-5, Fitzmeyer; "Matthean Divorce Texts," 205-206.

42. Boring, "Christian Prophets," 516-517.

43. E.g. Sanders, *Jesus and Judaism*; Geza Vermes, *Jesus the Jew: A Historian Reading the Gospels* (London: William Collins Sons & Co, Ltd, 1973), *Jesus and the World of Judaism* (Philadelphia: Fortress, 1983); Alan F. Segal, "Jesus the Jewish Revolutionary," *Rebecca's Children: Judaism and Christainity in the Roman World* (Cambridge, MA: Harvard University Press), 68-96; Daniel J. Harrington, "The Jewishness of Jesus: Facing Some Problems," CBQ 49 (1987), 1-13.

44. See e.g. MacRae, "NT Perspectives," 7.

45. See the emphasis on Paul's pragmatic approach in O. Larry Yarbro, *Not Like the Gentiles: Marriage Rules in the Letters of Paul* (SBL Dissertation Series 80; Atlanta, GA: Scholars Press, 1985). Also on sexual norms and self- definition, see Vincent L. Wimbush, *Paul the Worldly Ascetic: Response to the World and Self-Understanding according to 1 Corinthians 7* (Macon, GA: Mercer Press, 1987).

46. Fitzmyer, "The Matthean Divorce Texts," 197-226, esp. 213-223.

47. On the question of whether the passage prohibits divorce or polygamy, see Rabin, note 1 on line 21, p. 17. See also Paul Winter, "Sadoqite Fragments IV, 20, 21 and the Exegesis of Genesis 1:27 in late Judaism," *ZAW* 68 (1956), 71-84.

48. CD 4.19-5.1. The translation is mine and is based on the text of Chaim Rabin, *The Zadokite Documents* (Oxford: Oxford University Press, 1954), 17-19. Cf. Rabin's translation (16-18) and that of Geza Vermes, *The Dead Sea Scrolls in English* (Harmondsworth, England: Penguin, 1977), 101.

49. On this see the discussion of the word I have translated "instruction" in Lawrence H. Schiffman, *The Halakah at Qumran* (Studies in Judaism in Antiquity; Leiden: E.J. Brill, 1975), 49-54. For a different view, see Ginszburg cited in Rabin, *Zadokite Documents*, note 3 on 4.20, p. 16.

50. Fitzmeyer, "Matthean Divorce Texts," 226.

51. Schüssler Fiorenza, *Memory*, 143.

52. Schüssler Fiorenza, *Memory*, 140-142.

53. Gerd Theissen, *Sociology of Early Palestinian Christianity* (Philadephia: Fortress, 1989), 8.

54. Gerd Theissen, *Early Palestinian Christianity*, 19-20.

55. *Memory*, 145.

56. The daughters of Philip who are described by Luke as prophets are resident at Caesarea, Acts 19:8-9.

57. Yarbro, *Not Like the Gentiles*, 93-96 and the literature there.

58. See e.g. Jerome Murphy O'Connor, "The Divorced Woman in 1 Cor. 7:10-11," *JBL* 100 (1981), 601-606, esp. 602-603.

59. MacRae, "NT Perspectives," 8-9, Marrucci *Parole di Gesu'*, 316.

60. 2 *Apology* 2.

61. Yarbro, *Not Like the Gentiles*, 1-2, takes this the granting of the case as an aquittal; this is less than clear.

62. See Schüssler Fiorenza, *Memory*, 145.

63. Fitzmyer, "Matthean Divorce Texts," 217-221.

64. For a fuller discussion of the meanings of *porneia* see Marruci, *Parole di Gesu'* 333-412.

65. Mark 9:42-49 appears in Luke 17:1-2 in a much condensed version. Luke may feel that this passage involves an overly, not to say grossly, material view of the resurrection. Luke 14:34 appears in Mark 9:50.

66. On the importance of this verse in the ascetic tradition, particularly the Syrian ascetic tradition, see Sabastian P. Brock, Early Syrian Asceticism," *Numen* 20 (1973), 5-6. On women and ascesis in Luke, see M.R. D'Angelo, "Women in Luke-Acts: A Redactional View," *JBL* (forthcoming 1990).

67. Berger and Nicholas, "ADULTERY," *Oxford Classical Dictionary*, 10-11. The Mishnah forbids the taking back of a woman divorced "for evil fame" (Git. 4.7).

68. Rousselle (*Porneia* 103-103) describes the risks to a husband attempting to put this into practice and also the difficulties of a woman trying to implement *Hermas'* policy.

69. See D.L. Balch, "Backgrounds of I Cor. VII: Sayings of the Lord in Q; Moses as an Ascetic *Theios Aner* in II Cor. III," *NTS* (1972) 351-364.

70. See on this Elaine Pagels, *Adam, Eve and the Serpent* (New York: Random House, 1988), esp. 3-77.

71. Kraemer, Ross, "The Conversion of Women to Ascetic Forms of Christianity," *Signs* 6 (1980-81), 298-307.

72. On the patriarchal character of asceticism for women, see Elizabeth Castelli, "Virginity and its Meaning for Women's Sexuality in Early Christianity," *Journal of Feminist Studies in Religion* 2 (1986), 61-88.

73. See e.g. Edouard Cothenet, "Les prophètes chrétiens comme exégètes charismatiques de l'écriture," *Prophetic Vocation* (ed. Johannes Panagopoulos), 77-107.

74. David Hill, "Christian Prophets as Teachers or Instructors in the Church," *Prophetic Vocation* (ed. Johannes Panagopoulos), 108-130.

6
Divorce and Remarriage:
A Moral Perspective

Margaret A. Farley, R.S.M.

There is hardly a family within the Christian community, even the Roman Catholic community, that has not been touched in some way in recent years by questions of divorce and remarriage. The reality or at least the possibility of the breakdown and loss of a marital relationship is close to hand in one way or another for almost everyone (whether for our relatives or our friends or ourselves), and beyond it emerges the inevitable question of remarriage. Of course, both of these problems have preoccupied theologians and church leaders frequently enough throughout the centuries that were we not faced with new and urgent situations we should weary of addressing them yet again.

Perhaps contemporary experience is sharp enough, and history long enough, for us to gain a perspective not heretofore accessible regarding the issues of divorce and remarriage. Yet the obstacles to new and needed insights seem formidable. It is not easy to know even whether we are asking the right questions. Life seems to have moved us beyond issues of simply whether the church should recognize divorce and accept remarriage, or even whether marriage can be in some sense indestructible no matter what. We cannot help asking, for example, what we are to do about the fragility of contemporary marriages and the trauma and sometimes tragedy of their collapse, and what we are to make of the complexities of relationships that come with second and third marriages and their resultant "blended families." What new forms shall marriage and family take as cultures meet and interact and change? What models shall there be for the family that fit the needs and desires of individuals and serve the good of society? What shall count as faithfulness, what be required for responsibility, what liberate for human flourishing in community? And as women and men strive to found and sustain marriages and families in the days to come, what clarifying or healing words has the church to speak, and what empowering grace to offer? We seek clarity on such questions because problems and possibilities abound, and in them may lie moral claims for us all.

Problem with Sources

With the questions that press us today, however, it is difficult to engage the tradition of biblical, theological, and canonical legal sources as they have standardly developed in relation to divorce and remarriage. Even traditional secular sources—of law, social theory, history, philosophy— seem only marginally helpful. When we look to any of these usual sources for moral insight within the Christian community it is almost as if we "cannot get here from there." One reason for our difficulty is that the traditional sources we might draw upon are lodged in the history of institutions whose relationships to marriage and family have often been ambivalent. In western civilization, marriage and family have been disciplined and shepherded by ecclesiastical and civil authorities. The Christian church and the state have shaped, sustained, interpreted, regulated familial relations. And while the church and secular governments have valued marriage and family, they have also been hostile to them; while they have supported marriage and family, they have also been their competitors—suspicious of sexual relations, jealous of the time and energy familial life takes, wishing to harness married love and family stability for purposes beyond and sometimes even against the good of the family itself. Dialogue with tradition, then, may in many ways be inadequate to the task of understanding contemporary problems of marriage and family—especially when the ideals and obligations bequeathed by the past are dissonant with the experience of the present.

But there is an even stronger way to identify reasons for pessimism about traditional sources for clarifying contemporary problems of divorce and remarriage. That is, we can say: How is it possible to gain wisdom from traditions that have made so many (now to us) obvious mistakes? Is it possible, for example, that we will be able to understand the relationship between wives and husbands if we depend in any way on traditions that failed for centuries to understand the reality of women? Is it possible to gain insight into the nature of marital union from a tradition that articulates human self-giving in terms of yielding to another a "power" over one's body? Shall we simply get caught in confusion by traditional formulations that make spiritual communion central to marriage yet allow remarriage after the bodily death of a spouse and disallow remarriage after the spiritual death of a relationship? The traditional teaching of the Latin church regarding marriage may have serious enough problems that as a major source for our understanding it presents distractions and dangerous pitfalls.

Let me take time to elaborate on this possibility lest it appear merely as a slogan, as rhetoric of suspicion not appropriate to our present enterprise. I am very serious indeed about the question of whether the traditions to which we appeal, or with which we dialogue, can only hinder and not help our search for understanding regarding divorce and remarriage (and our discernment finally of moral obligation in this regard). It is, or course, probably the case that every tradition of understanding and practice regarding marriage and family is marked by the deep speculative errors and moral wrongs of sexism, classism, and racism. It would be surprising if the problems of society in general did not permeate and influence the institutions of marriage and family within society.[1] All cultures and all religions no doubt must struggle with such distortions within and without. But insofar as a tradition generates, undergirds, or appropriates these errors, to that extent or in that precise regard it can hardly serve as a source of contemporary wisdom or moral clarity. This is true, it seems to me, in at least some respects of the tradition of the Roman Catholic Church regarding marriage and family. Two examples come readily to mind.

First, central to the tradition has been the notion that marriage is a sacrament because or insofar as it images and bears witness to the covenant between Christ and the church. The structure of the image includes a gender assignment of roles—the husband imaging Jesus Christ and the wife imaging the church. This has been, of course, consonant with beliefs about hierarchy in spousal relations, about a relationship of ruler and ruled, leader and follower.[2] Indeed, it has represented only one expression among many of the presumed inequality intrinsic to the relationship which is at the heart of marriage. Yet nowhere in the traditional theology of marriage has this inequality been more explicitly identified than in the analogy made with the relationship between Christ and the church; nowhere has it been provided with a clearer rationale; nowhere has it been fixed as firmly with the power of an unquestioned symbol.

Today, it is true, efforts are being made by theologians and church leaders to transform the structure of the image so that wife and husband can be understood to be equal. Karl Rahner has argued, for example, that there is no need for husband and wife to represent respectively Christ and the church in a relationship of "leadership and subordination."[3] Neither the elements of solicitude and obedience, nor gender-identified roles, are the central "objective factor" that is decisive in the analogy. What primary images, reflects, the covenant of Christ and the church is the *unity* in the marriage relationship, not sociological structures that are inevitably culture-relative.

Yet we must at least wonder about a tradition's capacity to dissociate the received structure of a symbol from the symbol as a whole. For example, few have followed Rahner's lead and most efforts have instead been only to exchange a hierarchical model of relationship between husband and wife for one described as "complementary." What feminists have learned, however, is that complementarity is the last protective barrier for hierarchy, for one of the complements is inevitably restricted in role and thereby still subordinated to the other.[4]

Questions remain, then: Can a tradition that has been so wrong about the basic realities of women and men help us now to understand the possibilities of relationship between wife and husband—or for that matter the possibilities of relationship that spouses have with God? And what insights are possible regarding divorce and remarriage from a tradition that makes the sacramentality of marriage a critical warrant for the indissolubility of marriage, and that makes the imaging of a covenant between unequals a critical warrant for sacramentality?

A second example of a serious problem in the Latin tradition regarding marriage also relates to the issue of divorce and remarriage. Central to the notion of what marriage *is* in the Latin tradition is an understanding of what it means to become "two in one flesh" (Mark 10:8, Matthew 19:5-6). Unity in one "flesh" has functioned conceptually both as explication of the sacramental significance of marriage and as an argument for the essential permanence and indissolubility of marriage. Logically prior to its functioning in these ways, however, it has had to have some meaning in itself. It has been interpreted variously to mean "exchange of bodies," "an exchange of the right to sexual acts," a giving of power over one's body to another, a total self-giving of spouses one to the other, a sharing of the whole life of two persons together.[5] All of these interpretations are deeply problematic in a moral evaluation of marriage as a relation between persons.

Some of the difficulties with traditional understandings of "two in one flesh" are fairly obvious. For example, any interpretation that focuses on "total self-giving" or on some kind of fusion of the selves of married partners must answer to charges that it is not ethically justifiable to yield oneself to another in a way that entails loss of autonomy or a violation of what is essential to human personality as such. While evidence can be marshalled to show that the tradition at its best did not intend this negative meaning for "two in one flesh," nonetheless the consequences of language like "total self-giving" have been different for women and for men. There is, in fact, little in the tradition that has not encouraged loss of identity on the part of wives, setting an ideal for the self-giving of women that is morally questionable.

Even more dangerous to women than this, however, has been the language of giving to another a right over one's body, yielding to another power over one's own body. Efforts to explain this in terms of a mutuality of giving have hardly mitigated the problems entailed by this notion's placement in a context where husbands have been assumed to be active and wives to be primarily passive. It still must be said that chosen or enforced loss of agency in regard to one's own body, apart even from its vulnerability to terrible abuse, is not morally justifiable. The fact that the tradition has supported or even tolerated such notions in its analyses of the "marriage debt," in its interpretation of the differences between male and female sexuality, in its pastoral guidance especially of women, gives us pause when it comes to taking seriously the concept of "two in one flesh" as a theological ground for the indissolubility of marriage.

Closely aligned with this troubling issue is the longstanding conviction in the tradition that absolute indissolubility is achieved when marriage is not only consented to and vowed between partners, but "consummated" by them through sexual intercourse. When the two become "one flesh" in this sense, then the marriage is indissoluble and imperishable.[6] While anyone can appreciate the genuine struggle in the tradition to discern what it means for marriage to be constituted as a sharing of life that includes embodiment specifically as sexual, it is hardly credible today to make the permanence of marriage rest even in part on the sheer fact of one experience of sexual intercourse. But my point here is not so much to question this judgement in the tradition (for others have done so effectively and frequently) as to question what lies behind it.

There are, of course, ways in which sexual activity can be understood to complete and to symbolize a commitment two people are trying to express. And there surely are ways in which sexual activity is bonding in an ongoing relationship. There are even good reasons to argue that a sexual relationship requires permanent commitment between persons for its own dynamism to be honored and for persons to be radically respected.[7] All of this notwithstanding, there is a question difficult to avoid: Does the massive moral weight given to one sexual experience at the beginning of marriage suggest that the driving force in the tradition behind a doctrine of marital indissolubility is an ongoing primary concern for sexual purity? That is to say, may a marriage never be ended, and a remarriage never be undertaken, because it is forbidden that a person share her or his body with more than one other? because it is not to be imagined that once joined sexually with one person, one could legitimately be joined sexually with another? because sexuality is finally not in the service of relationship, but in the continuing economy of purity and defilement?[8] If such questions are both intelligible to us and unavoidable, they suggest a need for more than the traditional hermeneutical vantage points for interpreting the tradition.

I began my considerations of problems in the Roman Catholic tradition regarding marriage and family, and regarding divorce and remarriage, with a concern for the usefulness of traditional resources for addressing our questions of today. The viability of any ethical tradition depends, of course, on its doing something more than making mistakes about basic realities or promoting ideas that oppress. My own conviction about the Roman Catholic tradition is that it remains a viable tradition despite its mistakes and its oppression, but that what is useful in it specifically for our questions regarding divorce and remarriage cannot be found without a "hermeneutic of suspicion"[9] for its explicit teachings on sexuality and on marriage, and without looking beyond these teachings in the tradition for other resources that are relevant to marriage and to family.

Continuity but Reconstruction

What I want to do now is in a sense to begin looking elsewhere in the tradition, but my task is not primarily an historical one. Rather, I take now as my starting point the conviction deep in the tradition that the moral life of persons is supposed to "make sense." That is, what we ought to do and be can be understood by us at least in its basic obligations and possibilities. The Roman Catholic tradition of moral theology and ethics has not been premised on a "divine command" theory of obligation but on a theory of natural law both reasoned and revealed. This has taken many forms, but at its heart is the presupposition that there is something to be found in the reality of things, of persons and relations, that gives rise to moral obligation. Revelation is necessary for many of our moral findings, but revelation functions precisely to help us make sense of our lives both natural and graced.[10] Mediation of insight by persons of wisdom and communal authority may be necessary to us in some spheres of human action, but the goal of our searches is understanding not submission to doctrine or law. No matter what our sources of insight, we have limited access to reality, but that is a condition we all share. Our understandings are to an important extent historical and socially constructed, but that gives us a many-sided task and perhaps a salutary epistemological humility.

We undertake discernment today regarding questions of marriage and family in a very different social and cultural context than those out of which most traditional teachings and discipline have come. We are not struggling to affirm the goodness of marriage and sex against movements that denigrate it or that advocate radical forms of asceticism. But like the tradition before us, central to our efforts to "make sense" of marriage (and of divorce in relation to it) is the need to make sense of the commitment that is at its heart. Whatever the permutations in traditional definitions of the nature of marriage, there is a strong and consistent agreement throughout the centuries and into the present time that the mutual consent of partners is essential to marriage, and this consent is a covenanting, a committing, consent to relationship. "The intimate partnership of married life and love . . . is rooted in the conjugal covenant of irrevocable personal consent."[11]

Marriage is, of course, a unique kind of human commitment, but it partakes of the meaning and functions, limitations and possibilities of commitment in general. Hence, important light can be shed on it, and on divorce and remarriage, by examining the meaning of commitment, the purposes of commitment, and criteria for continuing obligation or justified release from commitment.

The Commitment to Marry

If marriage essentially involves a commitment, and if a commitment obligates, morally binds, the one who makes it, then any moral or ethical assessment of divorce must begin with a consideration of the commitment to marry. Much of what is important about this commitment is contained in the meaning of commitment as such. But what, indeed, does it mean to make a commitment?[12]

Commitments made to persons are sometimes called promises. When we promise someone something, we say that we "give our word." But what do we give when we "give our word"? First, we do something, or aim to do something, that relates to the future. We promise to do something or be something in relation to someone in the future. We are not simply *predicting* that we will do or be this (though prediction is also a way of relating to the future); for commitment implies obligation and responsibility for the future in a way that prediction does not. Nor are we simply *resolving* by and in ourselves to do something in the future (though resolution also relates to the future); for resolution may involve only an obligation to be consistent with our own choices. Rather, commitment entails giving our word in the sense of yielding to another a *claim* over ourselves—a claim to be and to do what we have promised. Hence, commitment includes at least two specific elements: an intention regarding future action (which may include interior actions like love, belief, etc.) and a putting of ourselves under a moral claim regarding that action.

What happens, then, when we make a commitment is that we enter a new form of relationship. The root meaning of "commitment" lies in the Latin word *mittere*, "to send." We "send" our word into another. Other usages of the word "commitment" make this even clearer—as, for example, when we speak of "committing to the earth," or "committing to prison," or "committing to memory." To "commit" is to entrust, to "consign to a person's care" (as in the Oxford dictionary's reference to "committing all thy cares to God"). When we make a commitment, somehow we "place" ourselves in the other to whom we give our word.

When we give our word we often search for ways to "incarnate," to "concretize," to make tangible the word itself. For example, we sign our name. Our word within a contract is sealed by placing ourselves in the form of our name, written by our own hand, on the document. In an ancient Syrian form of blood-covenanting, one party was required to write her or his name in blood on a piece of animal skin which was then rolled and worn on the arm of the covenant partner. Other rites of blood-covenanting have gone even further, attempting to mingle the blood of the person with another. For blood was the sign of life, and it was one's life that was entrusted to the other in a sacred self-binding ritual.

What commitment means, then, and what it entails, is a new relation in the *present*—a relation of binding and being bound, giving and being claimed; but the commitment points to the *future*. The whole reason for the present relation *as obligating* is to try to influence the future. Indeed, what happens in the present (in the making of a commitment) is that a new relationship begins (one that includes being bound to my word in the other). But it is this relationship that now moves into the future—a relationship in which my word now calls to me from the other to whom I have given it.

Now to apply this meaning of commitment to marriage at least three observations are important. First, the commitment to marry seems to involve a commitment to more than one person. A commitment clearly is made by each marriage partner to the other. But in a Christian construal of what marriage is a commitment is also made to God and to a community of persons (to the church and to the wider society). The issues of faithfulness in these multiple directions will be different, and none of them can be ignored when we undertake considerations of whether or not a marriage commitment can be changed or released.

Secondly, while a commitment to marry is made to persons, its content includes a commitment to a certain framework of life in relation to persons. That is, while those who marry commit themselves to love one another, they do so by committing themselves to whatever is understood to be the institution, the framework of life, that is marriage.[13] "Framework," of course, has more than one level of meaning in the context of commitment. There is the level at which "marriage" (like "friendship" or "religious congregation") is a framework that structures a relationship into a generic form. There is also the level where framework means a certain cultural model of marriage (or friendship or religious community), as when marriage, for example, is based on a patriarchal model or on a model of partnership between equals. And finally there is the level of framework which is the particular structure worked out by particular participants in any relationship. In most commitments to marry, the commitment to marriage as a framework is explicit regarding the first level of meaning and implicit regarding the second and third (indeed, often with an unconscious equating of the first with the second).

Thirdly, the yielding of a claim over one's self, over one's future actions, does not in itself entail a morally questionable form of self-giving whereby one yields one's very identity or what is essential to human personality as such. Indeed, it is possible to make a commitment in which one promises one's whole future, all of one's love, even one's life, without violating the very nature of the self. For to give to another a claim over one's self is to exercise agency and to undertake a future obligation as an agent; it is not to abdicate responsibility for self-determination or to diminish oneself to the point of incapacity for personal relationship (or at least it need not, in principle, be so). The implication of this may become clearer if we move now to a consideration of why persons may be moved to make commitments, and why in particular they may wish to commit themselves to marriage. An important part of this consideration must be why a commitment to marry includes a commitment to permanence in relation.

The Commitment to Permanence Within the Commitment to Marry

Despite the massive changes in social contexts throughout the development of the tradition regarding marriage and family, reasons for incorporating an intention of permanent relationship into the essence of marital commitment are not radically different today than they have always been. The importance of interpersonal reasons has grown, it is true, and institutional reasons have receded. But there have always been reasons intrinsic to the relationship itself and reasons of social utility beyond the relationship. A way to begin to see these reasons is to look first to the basic reasons why we make any commitments at all.

The primary purpose of explicit, expressed interpersonal and social commitments is to provide some reliability of expectation regarding the actions of free persons whose wills are shakable.[14] It is to allow us some grounds for counting on one another. Commitment in the human community implies a state of affairs in which there is doubt about our future actions; it implies the possibility of failure to do in the future what we intend to do in the present. Hence, we give our word to one another as a way to assure others that we will be consistent and as a way to strengthen ourselves for fulfilling our present intentions in an otherwise uncertain future. Giving to someone a claim over our future actions provides a barrier against our fickle changes of heart. By commitment we undertake a new obligation; we give ourselves bonds (and give others power) which will help us to do what we truly want to do, but might otherwise not do, in the future.

Insofar as making commitments, making promises, provides assurance to others and strength to ourselves, it facilitates important aspects of human living. It is a device upon which personal relationships depend and which social life requires. By it we gain important goods and provide for social stability. But there is another reason why we make commitments, indeed why we make some of the most significant commitments in our lives. That is, we perceive that commitment can serve love. Like commitments generally, a commitment to love can hold us to our love, safeguard us from inconsistency, assure a beloved of our willingness to be held even to a claim on our love. Moreover, sometimes love desires to be whole, to gather up all of its future in a way that seems impossible to persons whose lives are stretched out in time. Commitment is a way to try to make love whole—to make it irrevocable and to communicate it so.

Now, of course, even commitment has not the power to wrap up our future or our freedom once and for all. To undertake an obligation in the present, to enter a new relationship in the present, moves us into the future in a way that we who are in this relationship are changed. But we are changed because we are now obligated, not because we are necessitated, to do what we have promised. Hence, we are sometimes moved not only to promise love but to tie our commitments to love to certain frameworks for love (frameworks like marriage). We want to give our love a future by embodying it in a framework that makes ongoing demands upon us, that allows us to share our lives in particular ways, that provides a context in which love may develop and intimacy may grow. Our hope is that in and by such a framework our love will endure and flourish and find its ways of fruitfulness.

Reasons for wanting commitment and commitment to permanence, then, can have to do with reasons of love. And there are further reasons for incorporating an intention to permanence within our understanding of marriage, reasons which may or may not be part of the motivation of individual persons who marry. That is to say, marriage as a social institution has "reasons for being" that (at least in Christian interpretations) seem to call for an intention to permanence. These reasons include the good of offspring (who will be better served by being reared in a stable context); the general good of society (which depends on the institutions within it, perhaps particularly the family, for its own ongoing stability and security); and the good of the church (in which marriage functions as a way of Christian life, a way of loving God and one's neighbor, and a sign of God's presence to all).

There is yet another reason for permanence in marriage that participates both in the reasons of love and in the reasons of social utility. Some interpreters of the nature and possibilities of human sexuality have argued that sex itself is best served by being activated in a context of commitment and of commitment that intends to be permanent.[15] In the past this was argued on the basis of the need to discipline sexuality, to give it a framework as a remedy for its otherwise dangerous and indomitable power. In our present experience, arguments are more frequently directed to the need to integrate sex into the whole of human love[16] or to give it a context in which it can be nurtured (rather than simply disciplined).[17]

Given any or all of these reasons for commitment to marriage, and given the nature of the commitment itself, is it possible to discern any circumstances or reasons which would justify its dissolution? Given any or all of these reasons for permanence in marriage, and the nature of the marital commitment itself, is it ever possible to justify its ending short of death? These are the questions that are intrinsic to our moral evaluation of divorce and of remarriage.

Release from the Permanent Obligation to Marriage

The fact that a moral obligation follows from making a commitment to another person or persons is evident in the very meaning of commitment. We are indeed bound by our word. We are, by our word, obligated to do what we have said we would do. We, by commitment, "undertake" a moral obligation. Despite this, very few of us would insist that the obligation resulting from every commitment is absolute. But is it absolute when it is a commitment to marry?

My own position is that while a marriage commitment, like all commitments, does indeed obligate us by reason of what it is and what it serves, nonetheless sometimes this obligation does not (as an obligation specifically to a marriage) "hold." We are used to accepting release from obligation when it can be determined that some basic flaw marked the original marriage promises—a flaw in the procedure or a lack of capacity to promise in one or both of the partners or a fundamental inability to implement a married life from the beginning. Strictly speaking this kind of release from obligation is, as we know, not a "release" but a determination that no real marriage obligation was ever undertaken; the marriage never really existed. Insofar as this is an accurate determination in a given situation, it indicates not that the commitment no longer binds but that it was in an important sense invalid, and hence nonbinding, all along.

The question we need to press, however, is whether and on what basis a truly *valid* marriage may no longer bind. What shall we say of situations in which things simply have changed since the original commitment was made? Both partners have changed, the relationship between them has changed, and the original reason for the commitment seems altogether gone. The point of the commitment, of course, was to bind together those who made it in spite of any changes that might come. But now can it hold? Can it now really hold absolutely, in the face of radical change?

I could at this point consider changes like those traditionally identified in relation to the Pauline and Petrine "privileges." I prefer, however, to reflect more generically on the sorts of changes that appear to justify a release from the commitment-obligation of marriage.[18] There are three situations, it seems to me, in which it is indeed possible for things to change within or surrounding a commitment-relationship (even of marriage) so that the claim intrinsic to the commitment can be released. These are situations in which (1) it truly becomes *impossible* to keep the commitment; (2) the commitment-obligation no longer fulfills the *purposes* it was meant to serve; (3) another obligation comes into *conflict* with, and takes priority over, the commitment-obligation in question (that is, the obligation to the marriage).[19] It is an extremely complex matter to discern when such situations actually exist, and the most that I can do here is to point to what is in some way involved.

First, then, when it truly becomes impossible to sustain a commitment-relationship, it may be justifiable to change it. Impossibility of fulfillment has long been accepted as a general justifying reason for release from the obligation of a promise. Theologians, for example, counseled Christians in the Middle Ages that they were not obligated to carry out the pilgrimages they had vowed to make if, in fact, the shrine to which they intended to go had been destroyed. Most of us have no difficulty recognizing our release from a commitment when we are physically unable to keep it (for example, my release from a promise to go hiking with a friend if I break my leg in the meantime). But, of course, the kind of impossibility we are concerned with in regard to marriage is not physical impossibility but psychological or moral impossibility. Determining when it is truly impossible to sustain a marriage in this sense is less like recognizing a clear and incontrovertible fact than it is like making a judgement and even a decision—hence our difficulty in discerning it.

Still, we do know examples of impossibility in this regard. A marriage relationship may have deteriorated so drastically that reconciliation is indeed impossible. No amount of effort seems able to heal the rupture between persons. What was once love is now bitterness and hatred, and remaining together threatens utter destruction to themselves and to others. Or some aspects of the relationship may still survive but others prove so contradictory to marriage that at least one partner can no longer sustain it (as, for example, in a situation of relentless domestic violence). Or terrible apathy and despair burden a person and a relationship so that unless there is drastic change one feels one will die. Or a new love arises and one reaches a point where it is impossible to "turn back" and restore the former relation. Whatever might have been done (and even ought to have been done) in the beginning of this new love, it is now too late to let it go.

In cases such as these we know how difficult it is to make a judgement of "impossibility." Why, we may say, cannot two people in situations such as these draw on their own courage and intelligence, with wise help from others, and find a way to be faithful to one another? Why can they not call on memory and hope in the original commitment, why not trust that new life will come after the desert of this experience? Or why can they not accept the tragic aspects of life and heroically let go of conflicting loves, remaining faithful to the life-long commitments they have made?

What is possible and not possible in every situation cannot be determined apart from the concrete experience of those who live them. Critical questions must be asked about the truthfulness of the analysis of any given situation and about the integrity of motive in those who are discerning and deciding. Nonetheless, it seems to me to be true that a "threshold" of real impossibility does exist, and that therefore "impossibility" can indeed constitute a legitimate reason for the release of some marriage commitments.

I turn now to the second reason on the basis of which marriages may no longer bind: When a marriage commitment ceases to fulfill the purposes it was meant to serve, it may be justifiable to end it. Perhaps a better way of saying this is that commitments may lose their point, their *raison d'être*, their own *intrinsic meaning*. This may happen even to marriages. In order to make sense of this, we need to consider just what *is* the "point" of marriage. I have already suggested that a commitment to marry is a commitment to love one's partner, but it is also specifically a commitment to a "framework" for loving—to marriage as a way of structuring a relationship, to a "married way" of loving. The *raison d'être* of marriage includes, then, the sustenance of a love, providing it with a way of living. And for Christians it is more than a way of loving a spouse; it is also a way of loving and growing in love of God and of other persons. The hope of those who marry (at least in principle if not always in practice) is that in and by the framework of marriage their love for God and for one another, for children and for neighbors near and far, will endure and flourish, be challenged and nurtured, and yield the fruits of love.

But if this does not prove to be the case; if the given framework for their love weakens it and threatens to destroy it altogether; if this framework (this marriage) turns out to block the love, because it places it in a shared life for which they are tragically ill-suited, etc.; then the obligation to this particular form of committed love, it seems to me, may no longer hold. The very commitment to love (in relation to which marriage has its meaning) may require that the commitment to marriage must come to an end. The meaning of every *framework* for love is finally relative to the *love* it is meant to serve.

It may be extremely rare that the whole meaning of marriage is lost or contradicted in a given marriage commitment. For marriage has multiple meanings in a way. Its *raison d'être* includes its meaning not only for spouses but for children, not only for family but for society and the church, not only as a way of loving human persons but of loving God. Even if it fails in one respect, it may continue to have essential meaning (not just important good consequences) in other respects. All of this notwithstanding, there are marriages whose tragedy seems to be that they are unable to serve any of the reasons for marriage; or whose contradictions in some respects are so grave that they undermine every other potential meaning for the marriage.[20] If and when this is the case, it seems reasonable to conclude that the marriage obligation no longer binds.

Closely related to this is the third and final situation in which a marriage obligation may end. That is, when another obligation comes into conflict with and takes priority over the obligation to a marriage, it may be justified to change or end the commitment to marriage. It is easy to see in general how some other obligations can conflict with and supersede the obligation to keep a promise. For example, if a stranger in dire need requires my immediate assistance I am not bound by my promise to spend an evening with my friends. It is not so easy to see what obligations could take priority over a commitment to marry. For marriage is one of those profound, central commitments in our lives whose seriousness of obligation is meant to override other claims almost without exception. It may not be possible, then, to clarify this kind of situation in the brief space that I have here, but let me at least point to some possible considerations in its regard.

It is, for example, possible that a given commitment to other persons could take priority over a commitment to marriage. Commitment to God, certainly, has always been thought to relativize all other commitments, and it has sometimes been used to justify abandoning a marriage partner.[21] Commitment to children can sometimes require the ending of a marriage. Commitment to the *wellbeing* of one's spouse may mean that ironically commitment to *marriage* to one's spouse must be let go. Commitment to a whole people who are oppressed and in need may take priority over commitment to marriage.[22]

Moreover, a fundamental obligation to one's own self (under God) may justify ending a marriage. This need not be thought of in self-centered terms, but rather in terms of the responsibility of all persons not to violate humanness even in oneself. Hence, if a marriage relationship entails the complete destruction of individual freedom, or if it renders one incapable of relationship in any meaningful sense, then it may be justifiable to end it. This does not mean that we are not called to a great and noble love that is self-sacrificing in a radical sense. But to sacrifice one's own self cannot mean to violate one's very human nature.

What may be coming clear from all of this is that while there are situations (of impossibility, loss of meaning, and conflict of obligations) in which the marriage-commitment may no longer bind, we are never justified in *not loving* someone—not a marriage partner any more than a stranger or even an enemy. It may even be argued that a marriage-commitment always entails a residue of obligation to one's partner—not only in an obligation to the sort of love which is included in the call to *universal* love of all persons (a call that Christians believe to be part of their faith and moral life) but an obligation to some form of *particular* love that is faithful to the relationship which at least once was (that is, the marriage relationship as such). We are called not only to an unconditional love of every human person (including a marriage partner), but a marriage-commitment may entail something unconditional about a particular way of loving—even though commitment to a *framework* for loving (to the relationship as an ongoing *marriage*) is not by itself completely unconditional or absolute.

This, however, leads to the further question of just *how far* we are or can be released from the obligation of marriage-commitments. That is, granted that there are situations in which divorce is justified (situations in which a marriage-commitment need not continue to bind), is it thereby also justifiable for previously married persons to marry again?

Release from the Obligation not to Remarry

If the issues of divorce and remarriage are separate issues, it can only be because when all is said and done about reasons for release from marriage-commitment obligations, a question remains about an ongoing obligation not to remarry. A Roman Catholic traditional analysis of this question favors the position that even if an end must come to a marriage in the sense of the sharing of a life (an end to "bed and board") there does indeed still remain an obligation not to remarry. But if it is justified, as I have argued above, to release partners from the "framework" of marriage, it may be that the release extends (at least sometimes) all the way to a release of the obligation not to remarry. Again, I can do little more here than suggest ways of reflecting on this question from a moral point of view.

If an obligation not to remarry were to remain even where a divorce can be justified, on what would it be based? Several possibilities come to mind. There could be, for example, a special stipulation in the original marital commitment that even if the marriage in all other respects ends, neither party will remarry. In this case, should it become impossible to continue to share a life together (and hence on the grounds of "impossibility" a *divorce* becomes justified), it could still be "possible" at least *not to marry* anyone else. The trouble with this as the basis for a prohibition of remarriage is that it does not seem to be one that is identified by the tradition or acknowledged explicitly in the commitment experience of those who marry in our society today.

Another possible basis for an ongoing obligation not to remarry is a revealed command from God. If it can be determined that revealed divine law makes absolute the indissolubility of marriage at least when it comes to freedom to remarry, then whatever our reasoning about these matters the issue would be settled. The trouble with this resolution of the problem is that we cannot ignore the exegetical questions surrounding the relevant biblical texts. This is why the Roman Catholic tradition has not argued that the issue is settled only on biblical grounds.[22]

Yet another warrant for a continuing obligation not to remarry could be the status of marriage as a stabilizing factor in society and as a witness to God's presence in the church. Here there are also problems, however. One of the central problems is, for example, generated by the ambiguity of a law against remarriage as a socially useful sign and the equally ambiguous nature of the witness of a prohibition against remarriage for the church. (Such a law within either church or society may sanction situations, ongoing "marriages," which in fact are countersigns to the stability of family relations or to the presence of God in the church.) In addition there is the problem of using individuals (whose lives may be marked by great suffering) for a purely social good—a good which may involve their own harm.

Then there is an argument against remarriage on the basis of the good of children. It is surely true that children can be seriously harmed not only by divorce but by the remarriage of one or both of their parents (harmed by ongoing hostility between their birth parents, by the complex configurations of siblings that may result from remarriage, etc.).[23] It is also surely true that parental responsibility to children remains after divorce and includes, insofar as it is possible, some shared forms of parenting—hence, some harmonious relations between parents. But again, it seems to claim too much to argue that in every case remarriage of divorced parents is more harmful than helpful to children, or that the responsibilities of shared parenting can never be fulfilled if divorced parents remarry.

Traditional Roman Catholic reasons for prohibiting remarriage after divorce rest primarily on different grounds than these; that is, they rest on different grounds than social utility or a special stipulation in the marriage contract. They rest, rather, on the belief that Christian sacramental marriage includes a kind of ontological bond between partners.[24] It is therefore argued that despite separation or divorce, a marriage continues to exist (that is, there is actually no release from the obligation to the marriage-commitment as such—only to certain aspects of its fulfillment). Hence, divorced persons are not free to remarry.

Reflection on the nature of the bond that is achieved through marriage is sorely needed today. How might such a bond endure despite the breakdown of a loving relationship, despite the breakdown of the shared life, the "bed and board," of the partners? For example, the question must be pressed as to how a tradition can consistently affirm an ontological bond between spouses and yet permit remarriage after the death of a spouse.[25]

I am not myself inclined to dismiss the question of whether or not a bond remains even after the seeming complete breakdown of the marriage relationship. In fact, there are many ways in which some bond does remain in the aftermath of the rupture of the relationship between two persons who were once married—whether or not one wants to describe this remainder as an "ontological" bond. What remains may include a "bodily" bonding (now experienced positively or negatively) as a result of the sexual relationship that once was part of the marriage. Or it may include a spiritual bonding (now experienced positively or negatively) as a result of months or years of a shared history together. If their marriage resulted in children, surely they are held in some relationship with each other in the ongoing project of parenting. In any case, the lives of two people once married to one another are forever changed by the experience of that marriage. Even if one spouse has been abandoned by the other, their shared past makes forever some difference (whether positively or negatively) in each one of their futures. This "difference," this continuing memory that somehow marks the being of each one, admits of degrees; for depending on the length and the quality of the marriage relationship, the change in the partners will vary.

But if some bond does remain—in spite of divorce—as a consequence of a commitment to marry and the experience of married life, does this bond suffice to sustain an obligation not to remarry? My own opinion is that it does not. Or, better, there are at least situations in which it need not. There are situations in which a divorced person may be morally free to remarry—situations in which the bond that remains from a previous marriage is not such that it prohibits remarriage. Whatever ongoing obligation the original marriage relationship entails, it need not entail the obligation not to remarry. Indeed, only a view of marriage within an economy of sexuality and purity may be able to sustain an absolute prohibition of remarriage after a justifiable divorce.

These considerations remain incomplete. Let me come to an end, then, not with final conclusions but with the sobering reminder that the shared task of Christian traditions is not simply to discern the moral justification of divorce and remarriage. It is also to search in the heart of our faith communities for a healing word which will help to strengthen marriages and to ease the pain of divorce when it is unavoidable. We know that there are ways we must not go in our efforts to prevent divorce: We must not return to situations of complete economic dependence for women; we must not restore patrilinear societies; we must not use the law (whether of church or society) simply to coerce or condemn; we must not turn sacramental grace into a prison for persons whose lives are at stake.

What we must try to do is to discern more clearly the "way" of marital faithfulness; to demystify sexuality even as we refuse to keep it in the economy of purity and defilement; to understand and to offer Eucharistic life to those who come in faith to the table; to help one another to hope in the Covenant that remains even when other covenants fail. What may help all of this is an ongoing effort to understand the commitments we make in marriage—their purpose and their consequences, their unconditionality and their limits.

Notes

1. For more than a common sense intuition in this regard, see, for example, the work of William J. Goode, *World Revolution and Family Patterns* (New York: The Free Press, 1963); Peter Laslett, *Family Life and Illicit Love in Earlier Generations* (Cambridge: Cambridge University Press, 1977); Jessie Bernard, *The Future of Marriage*, rev. ed. (New Haven: Yale University Press, 1982); Lillian Breslow Rubin, *Worlds of Pain* (New York: Basic Books, 1976).

2. For a particularly graphic example of this in the history of the veiling of brides in the wedding ceremony, see E. Schillebeeckx, *Marriage: Human Reality and Saving Mystery*, trans. N.D. Smith (New York: Sheed and Ward, 1965) p. 309.

3. Karl Rahner, "Marriage as a Sacrament," *Theological Investigations*, vol. 10, trans. David Bourke (New York: Herder and Herder, 1973), p. 218.

4. See, for example, the analyses of John Paul II in *The Apostolic Exhortation on the Family*, #19 and #25, in *Origins* 11 (Dec. 24, 1981), pp. 444 and 446; and *Love and Responsibility*, trans. H.T. Willetts (New York: Farrar, Straus, Giroux, 1981), p. 275.

5. See, for example, Theodore Mackin, *What Is Marriage* (New York: Paulist Press, 1982), pp. 186-88; also Schillebeeckx, *Marriage, passim.*

6. I am here assuming the context of marriage as a sacrament and the theological analysis of this in the Latin tradition.

7. See my treatment of this in "An Ethic for Same-Sex Relations," in *Challenge to Love*, ed. Robert Nugent (New York: Crossroad Publishing Co., 1983), pp. 103-104. See also John Paul II, *Apostolic Exhortation* #11.

8. For one analysis of the economy of defilement and purification, see Paul Ricoeur, *The Symbolism of Evil*, trans. E. Buchanan (New York: Harper & Row, 1967).

9. I use this term as it has been used by philosophers such as Ricoeur and by feminists generally.

10. I have argued this in more detail elsewhere, for example in "Moral Discourse in the Public Arena," in *Vatican Authority and American Catholic Dissent*, ed. William W. May (New York: Crossroad, 1987), pp. 174-75.

11. *Gaudium et Spes* #48.

12. Much of what follows regarding the nature and experience of commitment draws directly from my analysis in *Personal Commitments: Beginning, Keeping, Changing* (San Francisco: Harper & Row, Publishers, 1986), chap. 2. What I am trying to do here is to show the application of this analysis to marriage.

13. See John Paul II, *Love and Responsibility*, pp. 211f. Also, see Farley, *Personal Commitments*, p. 90.

14. Farley, *Personal Commitments*, p. 19.

15. The Christian tradition has held this consistently, of course, from Augustine's *On the Goodness of Marriage* to John Paul II's *Love and Responsibility*.

16. See, for example, John Paul II, *Love and Responsibility, passim.*

17. See Paul Ricoeur, "Wonder, Eroticism, and Enigma," in *Sexuality and Identity*, ed. Hendrik M. Ruitenbeck (New York: Delta Publishing Co., 1970), pp. 13-24.

18. For clarification of the "Pauline" and "Petrine" "privileges, see for example the comprehensive treatment in Theodore Mackin, *Divorce and Remarriage* (New York: Paulist Press, 1984).

19. Here again I am applying formal analyses made in *Personal Commitments*, chap. 7.

20. See *Personal Commitments*, pp. 94-99.

21. I do not mean to imply here that this has traditionally also justified remarriage.

22. See the interpretation offered by, for example, Theodore Mackin in *Divorce and Remarriage*, esp. chaps. 3-4; and Mary Rose D'Angelo in her essay in this present volume.

23. We are getting important information in this regard from studies such as Judith S. Wallerstein and Sandra Blakeslee, *Second Chances: Men, Women and Children A Decade After Divorce* (New York: Ticknor & Fields, 1989).

24. See Mackin, *Divorce and Remarriage*, pp. 516ff. I am not here considering explicitly the most recent developments that Mackin notes in his essay in this volume—that is, the shift from a focus on ontological bond to a juridical bond. My assessment of this latter basis for indissolubility will for now remain implicit in my analysis of the binding nature of commitment.

25. John Paul II argues that this can be explained in terms of the essentially this-worldly nature of marriage (though he also suggests that all other things being equal, it would be better for spouses not to remarry after the death of one of the partners). See *Love and Responsibility*, p. 212.

7
The Consequences
of Marital Breakdown

Jack Dominian

Since the early nineteen-sixties the whole of Western society has seen a dramatic rise in divorce which continued through the seventies and has plateaued in the eighties, although in the United States it still involves be-tween 40-50% of marriages (Stewart, Bjorsten, Glick 1985) and in Britain one in three (Haskey 1983). The number of men and women involved annually runs into millions. It is estimated that between 40-50% of children in the United States will experience divorce in the 1980s. By the age of 16, one in three white children in the United States will experience their family home being broken by divorce (Bumpass and Rindfuss 1979), whilst in Britain the figure is one in five (Haskey 1983).

The aftermath of divorce is seen and experienced by the spouses, their children, relatives, friends, lawyers, judges, doctors, teachers, clergy, marriage counsellors, and the place of employment. No one, however, sees the whole picture. In this way one of the most damaging social and psychological processes in society continues without anyone apparently appreciating the total cost and suffering to individuals and society. In this paper I want to redress this deficiency by looking at the wide ranging consequences of divorce.

Impact on Spouses

In order to understand the adverse effects upon the spouses, we need to appreciate that psychologically marriage has two characteristics. The first is the fact that marriage is an affective bond, that is to say that the couple holds itself together through emotions which are based on their mutual attachment. This attachment is the basis of the couple's emotional security and, when it is threatened, they experience psychological symptoms of — anxiety, aggression and depression. When we fear losing someone who is important to us, we experience first anxiety at the threatened loss, then anger and finally depression when we lose them. This sequence of events is translated into physical and psychological symptoms in the course of the couple's alienation from each other. Minor psychiatric symptoms of poor sleep, irritability, tension, anger and anxiety are complained of by men and women in the run up to their divorce. These symptoms may last for years—while the conflict escalates. Anxiety may lead to excessive alcohol consumption and increased smoking. The increased alcohol consumption may lead to disinhibition, conflict and physical violence. Another feature of the pre-divorce period is an increased incidence of depression. At work there is a loss of attention and concentration, and decision-making may become difficult. After the separation, there is not only a grief reaction of the loss of the partner but also an actual deprivation of the protection that marital intimacy gives to the couple. The health of the separated and divorced suffers considerably and the data give overwhelming proof of the assertion. Let us look first at the psychological evidence. Studies of happiness indicate that personal happiness is highest among the married and lowest among the separated, divorced and widowed (Bradburn 1969). At the other end of the scale is to be found psychiatric impairment. For both sexes the divorced and separated have the greatest psychiatric impairment (Briscoe et al. 1973; Briscoe and Smith 1974). In the range of psychiatric symptoms, depression is probably the commonest distress experienced. Anyone who has suffered from depression knows what an incapacitating condition it is and with it go lassitude, lack of drive and enthusiasm, loss of joy, inability to concentrate and a chronic inability to enjoy life.

It would not be surprising that the population of the divorced and separated, suffering so often from these symptoms, would seek medical help. It has been found that the use of outpatient psychiatric services by the divorced and separated is five times as high as for a comparable married population. This finding is backed up by a number of studies both in the United States (Rosen, Bahn, Kramer 1964) and in Britain (Robertson 1974). The next step up after the outpatient clinic is admission to a psychiatric hospital and it has been found that the rates of admission to psychiatric hospitals is ten times as high for the divorced and separated as for the married.

It can be seen that, in the immediate aftermath of divorce, men and women are psychologically disturbed and in particular experience depression. These individuals have lost their spouse and, if they do not have custody of their children, they feel they have lost them as well. For a period, all the principal markers of their life have disappeared. If they are fortunate, they will fall back on their parents, relations and friends, but if, for some reason, these are not available, they become some of the most isolated people in the community and they are prone to both suicidal attempts and to suicide itself. Most studies have shown that the divorced and separated follow closely the bereaved in having the highest suicide rate compared to the single and married (Gove 1973). The divorced also have high rates of suicidal attempts (Weissman 1974). The other self-destructive process, the increased consumption of alcohol and alcoholism, is most common among the divorced and separated.

All these problems are seen in the aftermath of divorce in the following few years, but the adversity does not stop there. When we look at death rates, these are worst for those who are widowed and divorced. Taking the average annual death rates per 100,000 men aged 15-64 by selected causes and marital status, we find the figures for coronary heart disease for the married is 176 and for the divorced 362. For cancer of the respiratory system, the rates are 28 and 65 respectively. Cirrohosis of the liver, which is indicative of heavy drinking, has figures of 11 and 79 respectively and motor vehicle accidents also show a marked increase with rates of 35 and 128. All these figures suggest that the divorced are a vulnerable group of individuals who are without the protection of an intimate companion and who suffer long term consequences as a result.

Death is not the only index of adverse effects among the divorced and separated. In terms of general ill-health and time lost from work, the divorced have a poor record. I quote here from a paper by Bjorksten and Stewart (1985): "The divorced and separated have the worst health status of all marital groups, since they have the highest rates of acute and chronic conditions, suffer the most partial work disability, take the most disability days per condition, especially for injuries, and have the highest average physician utilization rates and the longest hospital stays." Both by the criteria of psychiatric and physical ill-health, the divorced and separated have an extremely high rate of disturbance.

One Parent Families

Another consequence of divorce is the creation of one-parent families. In the United States in 1979, there were 5.3 million women-headed families, which included their own children under 18 years of age. These women suffer in a number of ways. Their income drops and the economic difficulties are considerable. These mothers often have to work and their particular difficulties have been identified among others by Weiss (1979). Single parents often have too little time to manage effectively. They have the responsibility of providing all the answers and decisions and they get overloaded. The combination of working, and looking after the home and the children leads to tiredness with the consequent irritability. Thirdly they have to provide emotional support for their children without having the means of recharging their own emotional batteries.

Remarriage

The single state following divorce is usually a temporary one. Most divorcees remarry; about five out of six men and three out of four women remarry after divorce. Those who are going to remarry do so soon after divorce. This often means that reconstitution families have young children of at least one of the partners, sometimes both, and there are of course, sometimes children from the second marriage. The dream of all those who divorce is that their second marriage will be a happy one. This is so in a number of instances, but detailed studies suggest that second marriages have the same failure rate as first marriages and in some studies the incidence is considerably higher (Cherlin 1978). The reasons for this are many. The presence of stepchildren increases conflict in the marriage. Unfinished business with the divorced spouse intrudes, and the visiting of children from the previous marriage can be a source of difficulty. Finally, there are the problems of continuing personality difficulties which are transferred from one marriage to the next.

I have referred to the adverse health status of the divorced and separated. Does remarriage help? The answer is that the health of the remarried compares favorably with that of first marriages (Weingarten 1980), but there are limitations. The remarried are more likely to use psychiatric and other professional services than those in their first marriages and to report greater chronic stress.

Impact of Divorce on Children

When divorce began to escalate in the 60s, one of the arguments put forward was that the children suffered from being in a household loaded with conflict and that divorce was better for them. The children's opinion was not asked; it was assumed that their elders and society as a whole knew better. In the last fifteen years we have had the opportunity to examine what divorce actually does to the children, independently of the conflict in the home. The evidence has shown overwhelmingly that, even if children suffer from a conflict-ridden home, they suffer as much, if not more, from divorce itself.

Children's Views

When the children of divorcing couples are asked for their opinion, it appears that they do not want their parents to divorce. These are the words of one study (Mitchell 1985): "The clear impression is that many of the children had experienced their parents' separation with disbelief and had longed for a reconciliation. Many had not considered parental arguments to be sufficient reason for ending a marriage. On the other hand, a quarter had been relieved when their parents had separated." The evidence from this study and others supports the view that children want their parents to stay together, preferably to overcome their differences, but, notwithstanding, to avoid divorce.

Early Symptoms

The two major studies that have been influential in this field have been those of Hetherington et al. (1978) and Wallerstein and Kelly (1980). The study by Hetherington et al. consisted of a sample of 48 white, middleclass, recently divorced families with a pre-school child and 48 matched intact families. Information was collected at 2 months, 1 year and two years after divorce. The findings indicate that divorce is associated with diminished parent performance, due to depression and feelings of incompetence, negative child behavior, such as non-compliance, nagging and whining and negative parent-child interaction with inconsistent discipline, decreased communication and decreased affection. These workers found that many of the negative effects had abated by the end of two years.

Wallerstein and Kelly (1980) studied 60 white middle-class families, with 131 children ranging in age from 3 to 18. They found that over 50% of the entire group of children were distraught, with a sense that their lives had been completely disrupted. In this study less than 10% of the children had been relieved by their parents' decision to divorce, despite the high incidence of exposure to physical violence during the marriage. Over 75% of the children opposed the divorce very strongly. At the time of the separation, two thirds of the children were touchier, more irritable and more unruly. The younger ones showed a need to cling, were more frequently weepy and some returned to bed-wetting. The young child's need to cling is connected with the feeling of fear that, if they let their mother out of their sight, she might not return. More than half the youngsters were experiencing a variety of depressive symptoms. Two thirds of the children yearned for the absent parent, who was usually the father, and the majority were lonely.

Later Manifestations

Five years after the divorce, one third of the children were still intensely unhappy and dissatisfied with their life. 17% felt rejected by the custodial parent, the mother, and nearly 40% unloved by the father. 37% of all children and adolescents were moderately to severely depressed and there was a whole range of manifestations, such as sexual promiscuity, delinquency, poor learning and a sense of intense and unrelieved emotional deprivation.

Generally speaking, two factors mediated for the better. The first is regular visiting by the non-custodial parent, who is usually the father, and secondly the absence of persistent conflict between the divorced parents. The study by Wallerstein and Kelly (1980) has shown that there is a substantial group of distressed children five years after divorce. This distress is deep, personal and invades the whole personality. These children are emotionally deprived and are hungry for love. This would lead us to expect that the adolescents would be craving for affection and, at the same time, would be wary of marriage. Research has shown that daughters of divorced parents have a heightened interest in boys, approaching promiscuous levels, yet at the same time they are suspicious and have less satisfactory dating experiences (Booth et al. 1984). Daughters of divorced parents tend to marry younger, are less educated and marry men with less desirable jobs (Carlson 1979; Mueller and Hope 1977). All this work suggests that girls in particular are hungry for affection, throw themselves at the first man, marry early and in doing so enter into the group of divorce-prone marriages. It has been amply confirmed that children from broken marriages tend to have a higher incidence of divorce in their own marriages (Hope and Mueller 1976; Kiernan 1986). As far as school behaviour is concerned, children from single parent homes have been found to have lower achievement scores and higher rates of absenteeism, truancy, suspension/expulsion and drop out (Lazarus 1980; Santrock 1972). A longitudinal study in Britain has shown that children of both sexes who had experienced parental divorce were likely to have underachieved educationally in their mid-twenties (Wadsworth and Maclean 1986).

These grown up men and women of divorced parents have been shown to be prone to depression and, as already mentioned in this paper, are more likely to need to see a mental health professional (Zill 1983). A recent study has shown that psychological well-being suffers in adults from divorced homes (Glenn and Kramer 1985). The authors conclude with the following statement: "The hypothesis is that the increase in the proportion of adults who are children of divorce in the next few decades will lead, in the absence of countervailing influences, to a steady and non-trivial decline in the overall level of well-being of the American adult population."

Public Cost

All that I have described so far is the private agony. There is also a public cost measured in terms of legal costs, social benefits paid out to single parents and the cost to industry through absenteeism. In Britain it has been estimated that this cost is of the order of two billion pounds.

Religion and Divorce

It is not often that a religious moral prohibition can be measured precisely in social and psychological terms. Divorce is such a one and there is no doubt that the social sciences are pointing out the high cost in human suffering of divorce. The time has come to recognize this and make prevention of marital breakdown one of the urgent priorities of Western society.

Prevention

How is prevention to be achieved? There are those who wish to put the clock back through a return to tougher divorce laws or an attitude in society which makes divorce behavior morally reprehensible. In my opinion, neither the law nor fear are suitable means of reversing the tide of divorce. The alternative is counselling, which can be effective if undertaken early enough. So often couples allow their marital difficulties to progress beyond the point of no return.

There is no easy solution but the following points are of importance. It is vital that society acknowleges that divorce is no panacea to happiness in personal relationships. The need to work and struggle for marital stability is vital. If couples are to overcome their difficulties, they need to be helped with their efforts. The real answer is that both the Church and society should take marriage infinitely more seriously than they do at present.

There is also a need for fundamental changes in attitudes. Thus the wedding must be seen not as the conclusion of the involvement of Church and society but the beginning. Marriage is an unfolding relationship which should be accompanied throughout its course. Children should be educated at school for personal relationships of love, which means much more than mere romantic love.

After the wedding, help should be available at key moments such as when children arrive and when couples experience critical periods in their lives. The parish should become the focus of support for marriage. Business should make it a point to assist its employees in the home-work interface and be concerned with the stresses that impinge on the marriage.

To sum up, couples need to be assisted throughout their marriage, both in the parish and at work, so that, when difficulties arise, these are negotiated rather than couples resorting to divorce.

Summary

In this paper I have presented evidence that divorce has a whole range of adverse and damaging effects on spouses, and on children, now and later on when they are adults. Children suffer extensively emotionally and scholastically, and as adults have lower socio-economic and educational achievements. Also their marriages are more prone to divorce. All this is the private agony; there is also the immense public cost.

References

Bjorksten, O.J. and Stewart, T.J., "Marital Status and Health," *New Clinical Concepts in Marital Therapy*, ed. O.J. Bjorksten, (Washington, D.C.: American Psychiatric Press, 1985.)

Booth, A., Brinkerhoff, D.B., and White L.K., "The Impact of Parental Divorce on Courtship," *Journal of Marriage and Family*, 1984, vol. 46, pp. 85, ff.

Bradburn, N.M., *The Structure of Psychological Well-Being*, (Hawthorne, New York: Aldine, 1969.)

Briscoe, C.W., et al., "Divorce and Psychiatric Disease," *Archives General Psychiatry*, 1973, vol. 29, pp. 119, ff.

Briscoe, C.W., and Smith, J.B., "Psychiatric Illness, Marital Events, and Divorce," *Journal of Nervous and Mental Disease*, 1974, vol. 158, pp. 440, ff.

Bumpass, L. and Rindfuss, R., "Children's Experience of Marital Disruption," *American Journal of Sociology*, 1979, vol. 85, pp. 49, ff.

Carlson, E.F., "Family Background, School and Early Marriage," *Journal of Marriage and Family*, 1979, vol. 41, pp. 341, ff.

Cherlin, A., "Remarriage as An Incomplete Institution," *American Journal of Sociology*, 1978, vol. 84, pp. 634, ff.

Glenn, N.D., and Kramer, K.B., "The Psychological Well-Being of Adult Children of Divorce," *Journal of Marriage and Family*, 1985, vol. 47, pp. 905, ff.

Gove, W.R., "Sex, Marital Status, and Mortality," *American Journal of Sociology*, 1973, vol. 79, pp. 45, ff.

Haskey, J., "Marital Status Before Marriage and Age At Marriage: Their Influence on the Chance of Divorce," *Population Trends*, 1983, vol. 32, pp. 4, ff.

Haskey, J., "Children of Divorcing Couples," *Population Trends*, 1983, vol. 31, pp. 20, ff.

Hetherington, E.M., Cox, M., and Cox, R., "The Aftermath of Divorce" in *Mother/Child, Father/Child Relationships*, ed. J. Stevens and M. Matthews (Washington, D.C.: National Association for the Education of Young Children, 1978), pp. 110-155.

Hope, H., and Mueller, C.W., "The Intergenerational Transmission of Marital Instability: Comparisons by Race and Sex," *Journal of Social Issues*, 1976, vol. 32, pp. 1, ff.

Kiernan, K.E., "Teenage Marriage and Marital Breakdown: A Longitudinal Study," *Populations Studies*, 1986, vol. 40, pp. 35, ff.

Lazarus, M., "One Parent Families and Their Children," *Principal*, 1980, vol. 60, pp. 31, ff.

Mitchell, A., *Children in the Middle*, (London and New York: Tavistock Publications 1985).

Mueller, C.W., and Hope, H., "Marital Instability: A Study of Transmission Between Generations," *Journal of Marriage and Family*, 1977, vol. 39, pp. 83, ff.

Robertson, N.C., "The Relationship Between Marital Status and the Risk of Psychiatric Referral," *British Journal of Psychiatry*, 1974, vol. 124, pp. 191, ff.

Rosen, B.M., Bahm, A.K., and Kramer, M., "Demographic and Diagnostic Characteristics of Psychiatric Clinic Outpatients in the U.S.A.," *American Journal of Orthopsychiatry*, 1961, vol. 34, pp. 455, ff.

Santrock, J.W., "Relation of Type and Onset of Father Absense to Cognitive Development," *Child Development*, 1972, vol. 43, pp. 455, ff.

Stewart, T.J., Bjorksten, O.J.W. and Glick, I.D., "Sociodemographic Aspects of Contemporary American Marriage," in *New Clinical Concepts in Marital Therapy*, ed. O.J.W. Bjorksten, (Washington, D.C.: American Psychiatric Press, 1985.)

Wadsworth, M.E.J., and Maclean, M., "Parents' Divorce and Children's Life Chances," *Children and Youth Service Review*, 1986, vol. 8, pp. 145, ff.

Wallerstein, J., and Kelly, J.B., *Surviving the Breakup*, (London: Grant McIntyre, 1980.)

Weiss, R.S., *Going It Alone: The Family Life and Social Situation of the Single Parent*, (New York: Basic Books, 1979.)

Weingarten, H., "Remarriage and Well-Being," *Journal of Family Issues*, 1980, vol. 1, pp. 533, ff.

Weissman, M.M., "The Epidemiology of Suicide Attempts," *Archives of General Psychiatry*, 1974, vol. 30, pp. 737, ff.

Zill, N., *Happy, Healthy, and Insecure*, (New York: Doubleday, 1983.)

8
Questions Concerning the Matrimonial Tribunals and the Annulment Process

Ladislas Orsy, S.J.

Questions concerning the matrimonial tribunals and the annulment process are raised outside and inside the Catholic church.

For instance, non-Catholics keep asking: Are you not granting divorces under the pretext of nullity?

Catholics keep asking: Is there even justice in the church when rich dioceses in the West can set up highly organized and efficient tribunals to help their own people while the poor dioceses of the third world cannot really afford them and must leave their faithful without help?

To answer such questions, and many more of them, a critical look at the tribunals and their operation is necessary. The term "critical" in this context does not mean idle criticism, but a detached examination in the light of objective criteria.

Should such an examination show that our present system falls short of an ideal, the question still remains if in the practical order a better alternative can be found. Such an alternative, to be valid, should display a good balance of values: it should eliminate inequalities world-wide and assure evenhanded and speedy justice everywhere. Also, it should be the occasion for a healing process for the men and women involved, and proclaim to the world at large the dedication of the church not only to the dispensation of justice but to the exercise of compassion.

In the spirit of Vatican Council II, which mandated that "there must be an on-going reformation in the church," *ecclesia semper reformanda* (*cf.* UR 6), it is right to face such problems and to raise even more questions, for the sake of a responsible assessment of our judicial system.

Practical changes may be far down the road, but they certainly cannot take place if they are not well grounded in intelligent and responsible inquiries—for which the time is now.

Methodology

There is no point in reporting again what can be found in the Code and in the various official documents of the church. They all speak of the tribunals as instruments of justice, which of course they are. That much is well known. The need is rather for approaching the issue from new and higher viewpoints, so that some fresh insights may emerge. Those insights, duly tested against the demands of concrete life, can eventually help us to understand and to improve (if so warranted) our ministry of justice.

My original plan for examining, with due fairness, the issue of tribunals was to follow the pattern of the usual procedure before a court: first, to present all the conceivable arguments in their favor; then, to move all the available objections, and finally, to pronounce a just judgment. But as I progressed in my reflections, I realized that the complex nature of the subject matter requires a more elaborate approach.

Thus, I shall organize my inquiries around four questions:

1. What are marriage tribunals?

2. What are the objective values the tribunals are meant to serve?

3. What are the subjective dispositions in the judges which contribute to the genesis of the judicial decisions?

4. Are there any possible alternatives to the tribunals?

My answers will not be exhaustive, but they will offer some further thoughts on a few topical issues, such as indissolubility, lay judges, and judicial delays.

1. What Are The Tribunals?

Their historical origin: the change from a pastoral to an institutional approach

The tribunals must be seen in their historical reality: they are not immutable fixtures but part of the evolving church.

The church was confronted with matrimonial issues from its very beginning; Paul's first epistle to the Corinthians testifies to that.

A significant change in handling matrimonial cases occurred as the system of tribunals gradually developed from the tenth century to the thirteenth.

In the first millennium the adjudication of marriage cases was somewhat informal: the officials of the church acted in response to personal requests, their aim being to help the persons in trouble "to save their souls." Their decisions or approaches displayed a pragmatic character, with more concern for living persons than for abstract principles. Such was the spirit of the patristic age: the operations of the church were dominated by a strong pastoral concern.

From the beginning of the second millennium a shift took place and the dominant preoccupation became the safeguarding of the institution. A standard and formal judicial process was introduced, and the procedure became dominated by abstract principles. It was a passage from the level of "Christian common sense" to that of abstractions; from a pastoral and pragmatic to an institutional and principled approach. The main factors in bringing about this change were the rediscovery of Roman law and the reception of Aristotelian philosophy in the schools. Both are masterpieces of abstraction.

Such a development should not be judged as a bad one; nor is it particular to the church. It is a normal process in history, including legal history. As civilization advances, there is more and more abstraction in every field of human activity.

By and large, the rules and operations of the tribunals have been inspired by civil law; the exclusion of abuses played a significant role in formulating them.

Today we continue to operate within the same legal framework and with a similar concern to safeguard the integrity of the institution of marriage.

The marriage tribunals are prudential institutions to bring forth prudential judgements.

The capacity of the tribunals extends only to the assessment of the external evidence: whether the proven facts point to the existence of a valid marriage—or to the absence of it. It does not extend into a supernatural world: no tribunal can say with final certainty whether or not the sacrament of matrimony exists. That fact is known to God alone. Hence the outcome of any trial is a reasonable judgement, formed according to known norms and with the help of human logic. Such judgement is fallible in its nature, but enough for practical purposes. It has a twofold impact: *externally* it either confirms or destroys an existing legal relationship (as the recognition of the marriage bond is either upheld or denied); *internally* it guides the conscience of the persons involved.

In brief: the tribunals are prudential institutions in the church; their task is to form prudential judgements. They are not institutions of divine law and they cannot form infallible judgements. Canon law clearly recognizes that much when it says that marriage cases are never closed, *non transeunt in rem iudicatam.*

2. What Are the Values the Tribunals Are Meant To Serve? (The Objective Aspect)

Every institution in the church has for its purpose the service of values, otherwise it would be a useless structure and an empty fabrication. Marriage tribunals are no exception: they have been introduced and kept for centuries in order to uphold certain values precious to the community.

It follows that if we wish to assess critically the existence and operations of those tribunals, we must turn our attention to the values they are meant to serve.

In the service of values

Naturally enough, the list of those values is not given in the Code of Canon Law; we need to reconstruct them. In doing so, we should remember that there is not always a precise distinction among them: not only do they complete each other but they overlap in several ways.

Institutional integrity. The sanctity of marriage is protected, irrespective of persons.

Doctrine. The church must uphold indissolubility. Once a marriage has been publicly contracted, it must stand unless it has been proven publicly that in reality it was not contracted. Any practical concession in this matter would be interpreted as a doctrinal concession.

Equal Justice. An impartial administration of justice requires that there be the same rules for everybody, and that courts operate in the same way everywhere, all of them subject to the control of a higher authority.

Fundamental rights. A just decision protects the rights of all persons concerned, spouses and children.

Legal security, for the community and persons concerned. Since marriage is not a purely private affair, the community has a right to know who is married to whom. Similarly, the couple and the children must not be left in uncertainty concerning their own legal status.

Truth. Experience proves that the discovery of the true state of things is well served by dialectical arguments; that is, by using the so-called adversary system. This system was developed and perfected over many centuries as an effective instrument in establishing the true state of facts.

Fidelity to our tradition. Stability is a value. A tradition of having tribunals should not be disregarded; the marriage tribunals date from the tenth century and have proved their value abundantly.

Instruments of development. In every case that comes before the courts, the abstract rules of the law meet concrete life situations. Out of this encounter a jurisprudence develops which in its turn has an influence over the evolution of statutory norms.

Opportunity for healing. The system certainly gives an opportunity to judges and advocates to make an effort toward helping the parties who may have suffered a great deal through the breakdown of their marriage. Indeed, parties to an annulment process often testify that it had a healing effect on them.

This list of values may not be complete. But it is certainly enough to show that the institution of tribunals is doing an important service in the church.

Values not well served

We must look now at the other side of the coin. First, in the operations of the tribunals are there deficiencies in the service of the values listed above? Second, are there certain values which should be served but are not?

The following is a list of those values which may not be well served, or served at all, by the tribunal system.

Personal pastoral care. The rules for the tribunals are not conceived from a pastoral point of view; the primary focus is not on the healing of the persons.

Doctrine. The message conveyed by frequent annulment does not support doctrinal integrity; quite the opposite, it undermines it.

Justice. In the concrete order the ideal of equal justice is not accomplished. The conditions for a healthy tribunal system exist only in the so-called developed countries where personnel and funds are available and there is freedom from state interference. It is unsuitable for other countries where all the energies of the church are consumed with the primary needs of evangelization or where it operates under severe restraints.

Fundamental rights. Some tribunals can become instruments of injustice by unreasonable delays that may deprive a person of a concrete possibility of getting married.

Further objections

The law has overreached its own capacity. The competence of the law extends to the external forum only; *there* it can administer justice. When in specifically psychological cases (as most cases are), the judges are required to determine (often on the testimony of third parties) with utter precision the internal state of the spirit of the petitioners as it was at the moment of the exchange of marital vows, perhaps many years ago, we cannot speak of precise justice in the ordinary sense of the term. In truth, in such cases the judges are more likely to dispense prudent pastoral advice than to pronounce a precise judgement on the objective state of rights and duties.

The canonical rules used by the courts in psychological cases reflect an understanding of the operations of the human psyche that is difficult (perhaps impossible) to uphold today. Canon law understands and explains the "intention" required for valid marriage in the categories of scholastic "faculty psychology," attributing specific and distinct functions to the "mind" and the "will"; a system which few Christian theologians, philosophers or psychologists would accept. Justice may not be well served by such a doubtfully valid system.

The procedure can cause serious psychological harm. There are always some for whom it is medically inadvisable to revive the memories of a first marriage that failed, especially if they had to go through a long period of psychological convalescence. They are not well served by the inquisitive character of a judicial investigation; at times their psychiatrist is absolutely opposed to it.

The expenses can be excessively high. The tribunal system requires an enormous amount of investment in personnel and in money, in time and energy. While the need for the evangelization of the world is so great, it is unfair to concentrate so much strength in the service of a few.

Now that we have seen the values the present system upholds and the values which it leaves without sufficient support, it is time to draw up a balance, that is, to form a prudential judgement on the tribunals themselves.

The tribunals proclaim a certain institutional integrity, sometimes more in their intent than in the actual message they generate. They are authentic guides for the consciences of the faithful, but one wonders if for the sake of conscience such a great apparatus and complex procedure is really necessary.

They can function well in the Western world; in underdeveloped countries they are often a failure for several reasons, such as the lack of means to set them up, the lack of personnel to handle the cases, a mentality not congenial to Western legal traditions.

Justice must be blind and must not favor any person. Indeed our tribunals are equally open to a person of contrite heart as to a person who is cynically seeking social acceptance. The evangelical mode, however, is different: Jesus came to heal the contrite of heart; he was not interested in dispensing justice to the pharisees.

3. What Is the Genesis of Judicial Decisions? (The Subjective Aspect)

Judgements do not arise by simply reading the information: they are conceived in the minds of the judges.

Here we are entering the field of epistemological considerations, an aspect hardly ever (never?) discussed in connection with the operation of the tribunals. The classical position, on which the approach of our canon law has been built, is that of a somewhat naïve realism, according to which it is enough to take a thorough "look" at the evidence in order to find the objective state of facts.

A more sophisticated and more correct approach is to admit that no human judges are ever able to achieve an exhaustive knowledge of the events which play a role in the formation of the marriage contract. They can only assess the significance of certain relevant facts, according to their own capacity to understand and judge them. They *create* decisions, and their personality plays a capital role in that process.

Two levels of operation

We must distinguish two levels in the operation of the tribunals: the level of gathering the evidence, and the level of interpreting it.

The gathering of the evidence. Evidence is gathered in the specific field that the law can reach; that is, through the presentation of external facts and events relevant to a given case. The primary and proper domain of the investigation of the tribunals is precisely this external world where facts and events can be ascertained empirically. This much should be obvious: to read the mind and the heart of people a divine power would be necessary.

The interpretation of the evidence. Once the evidence is collected, the judges interpret it in function of their own horizons, which ought to include an expertise in the law and may well include much other knowledge. They are not unlike physicians who interpret the symptoms in function of their medical learning and of much other knowledge that they may possess.

More on the interpretive stage

The evidence gathered consists of fragments which by themselves appear like the pieces of a jigsaw puzzle. They must be put together to reveal a consistent meaning. This seems to be the task of the interpretation.

But there is a difference between the image that emerges from the pieces of a puzzle and the interpretation that attributes a meaning to the evidence. The pieces of the puzzle can produce only one image, which has been there all along; the interpretation can bring forth several meanings, which are the creation of the inquiring mind prompted by the evidence. In other terms, the material image emerges automatically and uniformly when the pieces of the puzzle are put together; the judicial decision is the result of the insight of the judges into the facts presented to them.

Here the doctrine of horizon enters, and an important doctrine it is. It dispels the illusion that cases based on similar evidence will lead to similar decisions; and it argues the likelihood of varying judgements. Let me explain.

All judges have their own mental horizons in which they operate. When the evidence is presented to a court, their horizons play an integral role in finding its meaning—which is the decision. To illustrate and to demonstrate this, let us look at six judicial colleges, each with an additional new horizon. (Whatever we say of a college can be easily transferred to an individual judge.)

The horizon of the first college extends to pastoral care only; their deliberations are not subject to the normative rule of canon law. Accordingly, their decisions will be dictated by compassion and fairly immediate practical experience. (Did the church operate in this way during the first millennium when there was not a tribunal system?)

The second college is moved by pastoral considerations but they let canon law too play its part. Their decisions in a number of cases will be different from those of the first group; since they operate in a broader horizon, they can give a different meaning to the same facts. (Was this the way of the tribunals before the discoveries of modern psychology?)

The third college is familiar with theology and understands that legal norms are there to protect and promote theological values. Inevitably, theological principles and categories will enter into their deliberations. (Should our tribunals be open to such theological consideration?)

The fourth college's horizon extends beyond those mentioned to the field of psychology and psychiatry; their additional expertise will often determine their judgements. (Is it correct to say that the tribunals came to a new life, especially in the US, when judges began to pay attention to psychological factors, and to create new *capita nullitatis?*)

The fifth college has an additional sensitivity to cultural differences; in sifting the evidence, they may find a meaning that none of the previous groups could have detected. (Can a tribunal take into account ethnic differences?)

The sixth college understands well the corrective factors to the rigidity of the law: equity, *epieikeia, oikonomia,* and *lacuna,* and they are able to apply them judiciously to the facts of the case. They may see convincing evidence for nullity where the others could not have discovered it.

Such variations are not deviations; they are part of our human condition. They occur at every level of the tribunal system, and no amount of legislation can eliminate them. Although many studies exist on judicial decisions, to my best knowledge no study exists that would show how the horizon of the justices influences their sentences.

What is the impact of the decision of the tribunals?

Their judgment speaks to *the institutional structures of the church*, much in the same way as a constitutive law (determining the state of rights and duties) does: all the officials can act accordingly. There is legal clarity and there is legal security; both are important for a human community.

Their decision becomes a formative element for *the conscience of the persons involved*; unless such persons know of some overwhelming evidence to the contrary (usually confined to the internal forum), they can take it for secure guidance.

Can the present system be perfected?

The following suggestions are short on words, but long on actions:

*To begin with, there should be an honest admission that in some places the present system cannot work, or cannot work well; in those cases the law should accept the possibility of alternatives. The medieval principle *necessitas non habet legem sed ipsa sibi facit legem*, there is no law for necessity, it creates a law for itself, is as valid today as it was centuries ago.

*On the objective level: there should be a review of the values to be served; no mean task. One could go through the list of values as we gave it earlier and see what kinds of corrections are needed. Also, judges should be trained just as much in the doctrine of values as in the rules of procedure.

*On the subjective level: there is a need for the broadening of the horizons of the justices. A good philosophical and theological understanding of the nature and operation of the tribunals, in particular of the genesis of a decision, is necessary. Such knowledge transcends canon law.

*There should be work on corrective pastoral measures.

4. What Are the Conceivable Alternatives?

How to search for alternatives

Any proposal for a better system must satisfy two requirements: it has to be feasible in the concrete order and it ought to be inspired by ideals—a difficult combination.

The requirement of being feasible in the concrete order presents us with significant difficulties because the circumstances are so different from one place to another. To illustrate this, one could think of four dioceses: one in Western Europe where the judges operate within the horizon of classical canon law (mainly of the 1917 type); one in the U.S. where they work with a highly developed psychological doctrine; one in a missionary country where no personnel and funds are available for a tribunal; one in a country where the church is oppressed, the pastors have no free communication with their flock, and the government reads most confidential documents. How can one system suit them all?

The need for feasibility, however, does not mean any disregard for ideal solutions; they must be kept in mind as points of reference. We cannot do any sensible reform unless we aim for an ideal—even if we must accommodate our wish to the demands of concrete life.

Conceivable alternatives to the tribunals

A *preliminary note*: The tribunals developed in an age when the church was the guardian of the legal status of every individual: births, marriages, ordinations, deaths were recorded by the church. Thus, a consciousness developed in the church about the importance of a social order in which the status of every individual is clearly defined and recorded.

Today, however, most states have their own carefully kept records of the movement of their population and of the status of every individual. Church records are used for the needs of the believing community only.

A rather technical question is whether or not the church could accept some discrepancy between the official register and pastoral practice; this would be the case if a divorced and remarried person were admitted to the Eucharist.

Undoubtedly, the church cannot live by leaving everything to the "internal forum" alone; the institutional aspect cannot be disregarded. The issue is the wise balance between the two *fora*, internal and external.

A list of conceivable alternatives, with due criticism

One, there should be no official intervention by the church in marriage cases: the judgement over the marriage is left to the parties, counseled as they wish.

• There is nothing in our tradition to support this approach. The church is the trustee of the sacraments; marriage is a sacrament; the church is duty bound to take interest in it, and act as necessary.

Two, the church should intervene in a quasi-official way in the forum of the conscience only.

• The problem with this conception is that marriage can never be a purely private affair. A "domestic church" is a public "event"; the church at large has a public relationship with it; hence normally a public recognition of it is warranted.

Three, the church should intervene officially but not judicially; for instance by authorized counseling. A group of experts commissioned by the bishop could form a judgement on the validity of the marriage.

• The informality of such an approach could lead to an uneven pastoral practice in the church. Yet it may be the only possible approach in places where no tribunal can function efficiently.

Four, there should be tribunals but with no competency in matters concerning psychology or psychiatry.

• This solution would reduce the competency of the tribunals to cases where the external legal rules were violated. It is doubtful that such an artificial limitation of the admissible evidence would be possible.

Some modest proposals which are feasible without delay

• Continue to make the tribunals more pastoral.

• Investigate whether their operations can include in some way the reintroduction of the parties involved into the sacramental life of the church. (Repentance, reparation, new start, introduction into sacramental life.)

• Put precise time limits on the stages of proceedings. In this matter there is no need to wait for universal legislation (which has to accommodate the whole world); there is nothing in canon law to prevent a diocesan tribunal from announcing a policy of handling marriage cases (say) within six months.

• Introduce official alternatives to tribunals in places where they cannot work efficiently.

Further Questions, not directly connected with the issue of the tribunals but indirectly relevant

1. What is the correct meaning of indissolubility?

In the theoretical order, the matrimonial covenant can be subject to annulment whether or not it is considered indissoluble; the issue being the validity of the formation of the covenant and not its permanency.

In the practical order, were the dissolution of the bond admitted, there would not be much sense in seeking an annulment. History proves this abundantly in the case of non- Catholic religious denominations. Once they admitted divorce and remarriage, annulment processes eventually came to a halt. A striking example can be found in the history of the Anglican church in England.

In the Catholic church, writings and talks on indissolubility often leave much to be desired in scientific precision.

The correct way of stating the Catholic position is that no matrimonial covenant can exist without including explicitly or implicitly a commitment to the lifelong permanency of the marriage. This requirement is absolute; the church has never admitted any exception, such as a marriage for a term of years, not even in the case of the "natural" marriages of non-Christians. In ethical terms: the intention to marry brings with it the moral duty of commitment to permanency.

This absolute norm is balanced by the admission of certain remedial services through the "power" of the church, always "for the sake of religion." In the case of a marriage between two non-baptized persons, or one baptized and one non-baptized person, at the request of one of the parties the church is willing to terminate the marital obligations and grant the freedom to marry to each of the partners.

The same grant is available in the case of a sacramental marriage between two baptized persons provided that the union was not consummated.

In the Latin church no termination of the obligation is ever granted in the case of a sacramental and consummated marriage. Whether or not the church has the radical power to "free" a person even in such a case remains a "disputed question" among theologians and canonists. The issue is, however, somewhat moot because the Latin church has amply demonstrated that, for the sake of the common good, it would not be willing to use this power.

The church, no less than individual Christians, has the evangelical duty to uphold the stability and permanency of marriages. Its practical attitude then may well be the "radical" expression of a duty perceived as virtually absolute—because it is rooted in the Gospel. If so, this attitude is not more likely to change than a belief in a point of doctrine; there can be such a thing as a *belief* in a moral duty.

This dimension, as far as I know, has not been explored much by our scholars. (Cf. on this issue the Tridentine texts on marriage: how much of it represents a dogmatic pronouncement, how much is quasi-absolute moral stance?)

The question of indissolubility is often discussed in connection with the issue of the possibility of admitting the divorced and remarried to full eucharistic communion. I think that each of those problems is autonomous (even if related); the dogmatic question of indissolubility should be kept separate from the prudential issue of communion, as many theologians have pointed out (Kasper, Lehmann, Ratzinger, etc.).

2. Are lay judges admissible?

The argument against lay judges runs something like this: For a judicial decision participation in the "sacred power" is necessary,

Lay persons however cannot participate in that power, only "cooperate" with it (cf. canon 129 #2),

Lay persons therefore cannot give a judicial decision, only "cooperate" with those who participate in the sacred power.

On the basis of this or similar reasoning, no lay person can ever function as a single judge, but one (no more) lay person may be admitted to be a member of a collegiate tribunal of three provided the other two are in sacred orders. The former would be participation, the latter is cooperation.

There is a problem with this reasoning.

Is the judgment over the state of the evidence really an act of "sacred power"? Or is it the conclusion of a rational operation which can be performed by any intellectually qualified and responsible person? If so, no ordination is required to perform that task. Lay persons are no less capable to do it than those in orders. If "sacred power" is required at all, it is only for imposing the sentence; that is, to make it legally binding. If necessary, such a formal act can be still reserved to the bishop after the judgment is formed.

The fault with the reasoning against the full participation of lay judges in the judicial process is that it does not distinguish between two radically distinct operations: stating the truth and binding the subjects.

Once it is accepted that the forming of a judgement is a rational and not a "jurisdictional" operation, it follows that even in the present dispensation of the Code, there could be collegial tribunals constituted of lay persons, and there could be single lay judges.

There is, of course, a much broader question: just how far is the exclusion of non-ordained persons from the exercise of the power to govern a faithful representation of our historical traditions? I doubt it is; the evidence to the contrary is heavy.

3. How to handle unwarranted delays by tribunals?

Every marriage case is a request by the faithful for a judgement of an official agency of the church, the tribunal. That judgement has a double effect: it becomes regulatory in the juridical world and it gives a firm point of reference for the conscience of the parties. On that judgment important future courses of action may depend (to contract or not a new marriage; the education of children; employment, etc.).

Undoubtedly, the faithful have a right to address the church. Correspondingly, the church has a duty to respond, and to respond within reasonable time.

What happens if the response of the church is not forthcoming, or is unduly delayed (which means that the tribunal is either not functioning or not functioning properly)?

The answer is that when this happens, an apparent conflict has been created among the norms which should guide the conscience of the interested party. On the one hand (let us assume she is a woman) she has a right to an answer and a duty to wait for it; on the other hand she may have a right to marry and to do so within reasonable time (she wishes to have a child).

If it is objectively true that the ecclesiastical institution (the tribunal) is not functioning, the situation of the woman is not different from that of someone in the first Christian centuries having a similar problem but not having an official judicial court to turn to.

There is no simple and uniform answer to such a predicament; each case must be judged on its own merits. The strength of the evidence for the invalidity ought to play a determining role; further, the parties involved should seek advice from qualified and responsible persons.

If there is a genuine conflict of rights and duties, the problem should be resolved on the basis of the correct hierarchy of values and norms, the moral values and norms taking precedence over the legal ones.

Appendix

More reflections on method

The main title of this paper has the word *questions* in it for two reasons. The first is obvious and does not need explanation: it is an existential fact that many questions are asked about the annulment process, and to those questions we must give a fair hearing. The second is not so apparent and is consequently in need of some elucidation: it has to do with the dialectical method I followed in this inquiry.

Method is, of course, all important. A small mistake in the beginning can lead to a big error at the end.

Every good method is ultimately a determined pattern of operations which an inquiry must follow in order to produce reliable results. This is true in the field of any science, secular or sacred. The basic pattern of the correct method is rather simple: First, all the available information must be gathered scrupulously; second, the information should be interpreted with intelligence and creative talent; third, the interpretation should be rigorously tested and checked by being confronted with every conceivable objection to make sure that no insight survives which is not supported by the true state of facts. In other terms, true knowledge arises out of the crucible of a process where the three stages of assiduous research, intuitive insights and detached verification blend into a harmonious whole.

Now this method is relatively easy to follow in natural sciences, especially in the sheltered conditions of a laboratory. Besides, nature has its own built-in controls: when the observations are faulty, or their interpretation is biased, the experiment is likely to end in a disaster.

Such built-in controls do not exist in humanities, certainly not in theology or for that matter in canon law. For us theologians and canonists, it is relatively easy to stay with penetrating insights and propose them as the description of the true state of facts. The medieval scholars knew this only too well, hence they developed a dialectical method which made them verify every theory by confronting it with its contrary. Abelhard (early 12th century) was a great master of this method, Gratian (12th century) adapted it to canon law, and Aquinas (13th century) refined it for theological investigations.

We have nothing to lose and everything to gain by using essentially the same pattern: let every affirmation be tested by confronting it with its contrary. Truth is more likely to emerge from a healthy confrontation of propositions than from the advocacy of a thesis.

Thus, throughout this paper, I have tried to reason dialectically. At times this may have led to frustration: it did not produce a clear-cut answer. Yet, it may have brought another type of satisfaction: we know how complex reality is and how far we are from understanding it adequately.

The theological background of this paper

Canon law has only one ultimate purpose which is to uphold theological values. It follows that every practical norm must be conceived, explained and applied in function of some theological principles.

The underlying theological principles, however, may not be immediately evident in a canonical discourse. It is important therefore that canonists should account for their theological vision so that their practical proposals and reflections could be judged within their proper theological context.

For this reason I wish to draw briefly the reader's attention to the theological foundations from which my canonical reflections originate.

The overall theology of marriage that I hold and follow is explained in some detail in my book *Marriage in Canon Law: Text and Comments, Reflections and Questions,* Wilmington, DE: Glazier, 1988, which contains also an annotated and critical bibliography for further reference. As a more systematic exposition on the theology of marriage, I recommend the small but substantial book by Walter Kasper, *Theology of Christian Marriage*, translated from the German, New York: Seabury, 1980. It is not a comprehensive treatise but a second introduction into theology of marriage.

Concerning the much discussed Matthean clause on divorce, I rely mainly on an essay by Joseph Fitzmyer, "The Matthean Divorce Texts and Some New Palestinian Evidence," in his book *To Advance the Gospel: New Testament Studies*, New York: Crossroad, 1981; and on the major dissertation by Corrado Marucci, *Parole di Gesù sul divorzio*, Brescia: Morcelliana, 1982; both works distinguished by thorough research and balanced judgement.

A Final Note

Throughout these reflections, our questions and answers kept moving on the field of prudential decisions and actions. The very nature of that field is such that it never yields "the one perfect answer." It follows that often enough we must be contented with imperfect results. No harm will follow, however, as long as our contentment never includes the acceptance of faulty methods and uncritical affirmations. The tools of the inquiry must remain impeccable even if the product must be accommodated to the concrete demands of life. That is the meaning of prudence, and there lies the clue for future progress.

About the Authors

In her earlier years **Paula Ripple** was a high school and college educator. She also spent five years as a pastoral minister in a Minneapolis parish. What Paula Ripple, however, is most noted for is her work with separated and divorced persons. She served for five years as the first Executive Director of the North American Conference of Separated and Divorced Catholics. For the past fourteen years she has become a leader in working with the divorce experience and the recovery and adjustment process.

Paula has presented workshops throughout the United States and Canada for educators, family life personnel, and clergy of all faiths. She has directed retreats for college students, married couples, and for divorcing and separated persons. For several years she has been on the faculty for Retreats International and the Program for the Continuing Education of Clergy, both centered at the University of Notre Dame. She has also served as keynote speaker for National Marriage Encounter, the Gathering, the Mile High Congress in Denver, and at the National Meeting of Family Life Directors.

She has published numerous articles and produced several tapes. She is well known for her four popular books: *The Pain and The Possibility, Called To Be Friends, Walking with Loneliness*, and *Growing Strong at Broken Places.*

In February of 1985, Paula received the Assumption University (Windsor, Ontario) Gold Medal Award for their Christian Culture Series, and in 1988 she was recipient of the James J. Young Ministry Award from the North American Conference of Separated and Divorced Catholics.

Paula is married to Dr. Donald Comin and lives in LaCrosse, Wisconsin.

John H. Erickson is a graduate of Harvard College, Yale University, and St. Vladimir's Orthodox Theological Seminary (Crestwood, New York), where he currently is Assistant Professor of Canon Law and Church History and also serves in various administrative capacities. He has been a Robbins Fellow at the University of California School of Law and a Junior Fellow at the Dumbarton Oaks Center for Byzantine Studies. Actively involved in both ecumenical and church affairs, Professor Erickson is a member of the North American Orthodox/Roman Catholic Bilateral Consultation, the North American Anglican/Orthodox Consultation, and the Canonical Commission of the Orthodox Church in America. He is also the current president of the Orthodox Theological Society of America. His most recent scholarly publication is *The Challenge of Our Past: Essays in Orthodox Church History and Canon Law* (St. Vladimir's Seminary Press, Spring 1989). He hopes to complete a major study of *oikonomia* in the Eastern canonical tradition soon. Professor Erickson's hobbies include arranging and adapting Orthodox liturgical music. Married and the father of two children, he continues the Orthodox Church's traditional emphasis on the active participation of laypersons in church life.

Theodore Mackin, S.J., is a member of the California Province of the Society of Jesus. He received his B.A. and M.A. in philosophy at Gonzaga University, Spokane, and his S.T.D. from Gregorian University. His doctoral dissertation treated the topic: "The Instrumental-dispositive Causality in The Sacraments According to The Early Writings of Thomas Aquinas."

Since 1958 Theodore Mackin has been a member of the faculty of Religious Studies at Santa Clara University, where he specializes in sacramental theology and the theology of marriage. He is presently the John Nobili University Professor.

For almost three decades Father Mackin has been preparing a monumental trilogy on Catholic Marriage. All three volumes have been published by Paulist Press: *Marriage in the Catholic Church: What Is Marriage?; Marriage in the Catholic Church: Divorce and Remarriage*, and, *Marriage in the Catholic Church: The Marital Sacrament.*

Bernard Cooke received his M.A. in philosophy at St. Louis University, his Licentiate in Sacred Theology at St. Mary's College, Kansas, and his S.T.D. at Institut Catholique de Paris. For eleven years he was chairperson of the Department of Theology at Marquette University. He has been Professor of Religious Studies at the University of Windsor and the University of Calgary. He has also been Bernard Hanley Visiting Professor at the University of Santa Clara. Bernard Cooke is presently professor of Systematic Theology at Holy Cross College, Worcester, Massachusetts.

Cooke has published fifteen books and dozens of articles. Among his most significant books are *Christian Sacraments, Christian Personality, Ministry to Word and Sacrament*, and *Sacraments and Sacramentality.*

He has given numerous lectures, workshops, and summer courses in the United States, Canada, France, Spain, Switzerland, Japan, Korea, Ireland and East Africa. He is past president of the College Theology Society, and the Catholic Theological Society of America.

The University of Detroit bestowed on Bernard Cooke an honorary doctorate (Litt.D.). From 1968-70 he pursued a post- doctoral research fellowship at Yale Divinity School. During the 1983-84 academic year he was Fellow at the Wilson Center in Washington, D.C. At its 1979 annual convention, the Catholic Theological Society of America bestowed on Cooke its highest honor, the John Courtney Murray award.

Mary Rose D'Angelo received her B.A. degree in Classics at Fordham University, and her Ph.D. at Yale. Her area of specialization is Christian Origins. She has also done scholarly work in the history of interpretation of the Bible, Judaism in the Hellenistic era, and women in Christian antiquity.

Mary Rose D'Angelo is a member of the faculty in the Religious Studies Department at Villanova University. She has also held teaching positions in New Testament at St. Thomas Theological Seminary, Denver, at the University of St. Michael's College, Toronto, and at the Iliff School of Theology, Denver.

Professor D'Angelo is the author of *Moses in the Letter to The Hebrews*. Her other publications include articles on biblical interpretation, New Testament spirituality, inclusive language in the Bible, and women and the Christian tradition. She has also presented workshops in the United States and Canada.

Margaret A. Farley, R.S.M, a Sister of Mercy from the Detroit Province, holds the Gilbert L. Stark Professorship in Christian Ethics at Yale University Divinity School. She received a Masters degree in Philosophy from the University of Detroit and a doctorate in Religious Ethics from Yale University. She has taught at Mercy College of Detroit and at the University of Detroit. She joined the faculty of Yale University in 1971.

Professor Farley's work in the field of ethics includes a variety of activities and writings in the history of Christian ethics, medical ethics, sexual ethics, and social ethics. She has published over 40 articles in books and journals such as *Theological Studies, The Journal of Religious Ethics*, and *Horizons*. She is the co-author of a book entitled *A Metaphysics of*

Being and God, and her most recent book is called *Personal Commitments: Beginning, Keeping, Changing*.

Margaret Farley has worked extensively with organizations and institutions addressing women's issues, issues of medical technology, social responsibility, theological education, family and society.

Dr. Jack Dominian was born in Athens, Greece in 1929. After a period in India, he settled in England in 1945. He was trained in medicine in the Universities of Cambridge and Oxford. He was qualified as a doctor in 1955 and as a psychiatrist in 1961. He is now a consultant psychiatrist at the Central Middlesex Hospital, London.

From his earliest days he took an interest in marital problems. In 1971 he established the Marriage Research Centre of which he is the director.

His writings include *Christian Marriage* (1967), *The Church and the Sexual Revolution* (1971), *Marriage, Faith and Love* (1981), and *Sexual Integrity, The Answer to Aids* (1987).

Father Ladislas M. Orsy, S.J., a member of the New York Province of the Society of Jesus, received a Licentiate in Theology at Louvain, and a Doctorate in Canon Law at Gregorian University. Since 1974 he has been Professor of Canon Law at Catholic University of America. Prior to that he held professorships at Gregorian University and Fordham University.

He has authored nine books and over two hundred articles. His most recent books are *Marriage in Canon Law* and *The Church: Learning and Teaching—Magisterium, Assent, Dissent, Academic Freedom*.

Father Orsy is a member of the Board of Trustees, Marquette University, and of the Board of Directors, Georgetown University. The professional organizations of which he is a member include: Canon Law Society of America, Canon Law Society of Great Britain and Ireland, Eastern Law Society (Vienna, Austria), and the International Society for the Study of Canon Law (Rome).